SOCIOLOGY OF HEALTH

Reproductive Health Care and Social Exclusion-Social Inclusion

SOCIOLOGY OF HEALTH

Reproductive Health Care and Social Exclusion-Social Inclusion

By

Dr. K. Nagaraju
Deptt. of Sociology
Sri Krishnadevaraya University
Anantapur
Andhra Pradesh

&

Dr. Ch. Umamohan
Deptt. of Sociology
Director, Centre for the Study of
Social Exclusion & Inclusive Policy
Sri Krishnadevaraya University
Anantapur

DISCOVERY PUBLISHING HOUSE PVT. LTD.
NEW DELHI-110 002

Published by:

Tilak Wasan

DISCOVERY PUBLISHING HOUSE PVT. LTD.
4831/24, Ansari Road, Prahlad Street
Darya Ganj, New Delhi-110002 (India)
Phone: +91-11-23279245, 43764432
Fax: +91-11-23253475
E-mail: parul.wasan@gmail.com
discoverypublishinghouse@gmail.com
info@discoverypublishinggroup.com
web: www.discoverypublishinggroup.com

First Edition: **2011**
ISBN: 978-81-8356-731-2

Sociology of Health: ***Reproductive Health Care and Social Exclusion-Social Inclusion***

Printed at:
Shree Balaji Art Press
Delhi

Preface

In the light of the paradigmatic shift in the way population is understood in the post-Cairo era, it is necessary to integrate new areas of concern. Some of which include family life, gender equity, adolescent reproductive health. India, thus is seriously implementing a major paradigm shift in its family welfare programme. This choice represents a shift from the aim of achieving purely demographic goals to the adoption of comprehensive national development plan which incorporates the goals of the Cairo and Beijing international conferences on population, women and development. The concept of Reproductive Health brings a new dimension to safe motherhood, family planning and STD programmes.

In this context population health research has taught us that social and health inequality hurts everyone, not just those at the bottom. Similarly, everyone is hurt by social exclusion. - Therefore, the key association between social inclusion and the social determinants is social and health inequities (Health Canada, 2001)..Decades of research have further shown that social exclusion impacts health and is aggravated by health status (World Health Organization, 2005). Therefore, micro-level analyses of the links between reproductive health outcomes and their socio-economic and cultural antecedents in different settings would go a long way in tailoring services in locally relevant way.

In the light of these reflections, this book attempts to examine the social exclusion and social inclusion of reproductive health care practices of traditional communities in a chronically drought prone and backward district of Andhra Pradesh.

A number of colleagues and friends have provided valuable advice and assistance, hence we will be failing in our duty if we do not express our gratitude to them. We also express our gratitude to Shri Tilak Wasan & Shri Parul Wasan, Discovery Publishing House Pvt. Ltd., New Delhi for this manuscript in very limited time.

Authors

Contents

CHAPTER 1

Introduction

FRAME OF REFERENCE

In the light of the paradigmatic shift in the way population is understood in the post-Cairo era, it is necessary to integrate new areas of concern. Some of which include family life, gender equity, adolescent reproductive health, sustainable development.

In this context it is pertinent to mention that in July 1993, the Government of India set up a committee under the Chairmanship of Dr. Swaminathan to review the National Family Welfare Programme and draft a new national population policy. The Swaminathan Committee submitted a draft Population Policy in May 1994, four months before the ICPD in Cairo. The report contained far-reaching recommendations, amongst them one important recommendation being shifting the programme emphasis from achieving national demographic targets to helping couples achieve their reproductive goals. Many of the recommendations were consistent with the ICPD plan of action.

India is seriously implementing a major paradigm shift in its family welfare programme. This choice represents a shift from the aim of achieving purely demographic goals to the adoption of comprehensive national development plan which incorporates the goals of the Cairo and Beijing International Conferences on Population, Women and Development. The ICPD has helped in accelerating this process. As the first step, the method-specific family planning target approach has been replaced by a Reproductive and Child Health (RCH) Programme, which "aims to provide need-based, client-centered, demand-driven, high quality and integrated RCH services" (GOI, 1997).

REPRODUCTIVE AND CHILD HEALTH (RCH) PROGRAMME

The withdrawal of the target approach was the first step and almost an essential requirement for introducing the Reproductive and Child Health (RCH) Programme in India. The RCH programme was formally launched by the Ministry of Health and Family Welfare in October 1997. Essential components of the programme strategy included community participation in planning for servers, multi-sector approach in implementing and monitoring services, a client-centred, gender-sensitive approach to service provision, upgraded facilities and improved training, emphasis on quality of care, and the absence of contraceptive targets and incentives.

Operationally, the RCH Programme is an alternative integrated approach to the vertical programmes aimed at improving the health status of young women and children, which have been operating during the past decade. It incorporates all the components covered under the Child Survival and Safe Motherhood Programme (CSSM) and includes two additional components, one relating to sexually transmitted disease (STD) and another relating to other

Reproductive Tract Infection (RTI). Further, it emphasizes the provision of services in manner which is client-centered, demand driven, high quality and based on the needs of the community arrived at through decentralized participatory planning without target (GOI, 1997). Thus RCH programme seeks the efficiency of the earlier programmes, bring about a holistic approach to programme implementation and to produce a paradigm shift in implementation based upon client's needs.

CONCEPT OF REPRODUCTIVE HEALTH

"Reproductive Health is a state of complete physical, mental and social well-being and not merely absence of disease or infirmity, in all matters related to the reproductive system and to its functions and processes. Reproductive Health therefore, implies that people are able to have a satisfying and safe sex life and they have capability to reproduce and have freedom to decide if, when, and how often to do so. Implicit in this last condition are the rights of men and women to be informed and have access to safe, effective, affordable and acceptable method of family planning of their choice, as well as other methods of their choice for regulation of fertility which are not against the law, and the right of access to appropriate health-care services that will enable women to go safely through pregnancy and childbirth and provide couples with the best chance of having a healthy infant. It also includes sexual health, the purpose of which is enhancement of life and personal relations, and not merely counseling and care related to reproduction and sexually transmitted diseases" (ICPD Programme of Action).

A Reproductive Health focus provides a means for addressing health and population issues with an emphasis on needs of women and men. Specific reproductive events, notably pregnancy and child bearing have an impact on women's health as well as on traditionally emphasized demographic trends. However, Reproductive Health presents a life long process inextricable linked to the status and role of women in their homes and societies and is not just related to the biological events of conception and birth.

Reproductive Health is defined as 'the ability of women to live through the reproductive years and beyond, with reproductive choice, dignity and successful child bearing, and to be free from gynecological diseases and risks'. Within the framework of WHOs definition of health as "a state of complete physical, mental and social well-being and not merely the absence of disease or infirmity, reproductive health addresses the reproductive processes, functions and systems at all stages of life.

Reproductive Health implies that people are able to have a responsible, satisfying and safe sex-life, and that they have the capacity to reproduce and the freedom to decide if, when and how often, to do so. Implicit in this last condition are the right of men and women to be informed of and to have access to safe, effective, affordable and acceptable method of fertility regulation, of their choice, and the right of access to appropriate health services, that will enable women to go safely through their pregnancy and child birth and to provide couples with the best chance of having a healthy infant (WHO, 1994).

One cannot fail to notice that the concept of reproductive health has also been explained by a term reproductive morbidity. Various conceptualizations of reproductive health consider reproductive morbidity as inclusive of conditions of physical ill-health relating to 'successful child bearing and freedom from gynecological diseases and risks". WHO defines reproductive morbidity as "any morbidity due to dysfunction of reproductive tract which is a consequence of reproductive behaviour including pregnancy, abortion, child birth or sexual behaviour, arising due to physical, social and mental problems, or are aggravated by these functions". Zurayk, *et al.* (1993), also defined reproductive morbidity to include obstetric morbidity and gynecological morbidity, which include conditions during pregnancy, delivery and post partum period, as well as conditions of reproductive tract related infections, cervical cell changes, infertility and such other conditions respectively.

The complexity of the concept of reproductive health may seem overwhelming, particularly when translating it into action. The concept of reproductive health represents a new approach to existing programmes rather than a set of new programmes. It involves adapting what is already in place, revitalizing and modifying the same rather than starting from the scratch. An important aspect of the concept of reproductive health is the focus on meeting individual and community needs as the foremost priority. Also, this approach involves empowering women to take decisions regarding their reproductive lives; involving young people in the development and implementation of programmes and services; making greater efforts to reach the poorest of the poor, the marginalized and the excluded; and invoking men to assume greater responsibility for reproductive health.

Reproductive Health care is defined as the constellation of methods, techniques and services that contribute to the reproductive health and well-being by preventing and solving reproductive health problems. The essential components of reproductive health programmes include the following:

COMPONENTS OF REPRODUCTIVE HEALTH

A Reproductive Health approach links demographic concerns, including fertility reduction with a range of objectives for improving the health and socio-economic status of women. It also proposes to address the needs of special target groups such as adolescents, and to increase the involvement of men, and their responsibility, for sexual reproductive behaviour. Adopting this approach implies going beyond the domain of family planning to encompass additional aspects of human sexuality and reproductive health needs throughout the various states of the life cycle.

Prevention of unintended pregnancy through the provision of accessible and high quality family planning service which are based on reproductive needs of couples:

- Provision of safe abortion and post-abortion care services;
- Provision of safe motherhood services to improve maternal morbidity and mortality, including services to improve prenatal and neonatal mortality and post-neonatal mortality;
- Prevention and treatment of reproductive tract infections and sexually transmitted infections and HIV/AIDS transmission;
- Provision of reproductive health services to adolescents;
- Improving maternal and infant nutrition including promotion of breast feeding programmes;
- Screening and managing specific gynecological problems such as;
  - reproductive tract cancers, including breast cancer;
  - infertility;

The concept of Reproductive Health brings a new dimension to safe motherhood, family planning and STD programmes. Integrating them so that they are not delivered in isolation enables communities to deal in a more comprehensive manner in order to overcome the issue of territoriality.

CONCEPT OF SOCIAL EXCLUSION

Social exclusion is a concept commonly used in development, particularly following the World Social Summit in Copenhagen in 1995. Thereafter a number of multilateral development agencies, notably the World Bank and the International Labour Organization, adopted social exclusion as a multi-dimensional framework. It served to broaden poverty analysis and focus attention on both the causes and impact of social disadvantage.

Social exclusion is a concept that can describe, on the one hand, a condition or outcome, and, on the other, a dynamic process. (DFID, 2005).

As a *condition* or *outcome*, social exclusion is a state in which excluded individuals or groups are unable to participate fully in their society. This may result from: their social identity (for example race, gender, ethnicity, caste or religion), or social location (for example in areas that are remote, stigmatized or suffering from war or conflict).

As *a multi-dimensional and dynamic process,* social exclusion refers to the social relations and organizational barriers that block the attainment of livelihoods, human development and equal citizenship. It can create or sustain poverty and inequality, and can restrict social participation. As a dynamic process, social exclusion is governed by:

- Social and political relations, and
- Access to organizations and institutional sites of power.

Social exclusion does not focus on equality of outcomes but on the equal freedom to enjoy the rights of citizenship. In this sense, the social exclusion framework recognizes people's diversities in terms of their ability to seize opportunities, necessitating extra efforts by society to provide equal capabilities to all people. Thus, the focus is not on an equal starting point, or on a static assumption about who is and is not poor, but on the access to capabilities at various points in a person's life (Klasen, 1998).

Social exclusion stresses a process rather than a state allowing for an analysis of mechanisms and institutions as well as lending itself to policy design where problems and failures are identified within institutions. This represents a shift away from looking at deprivation according to individuals' attributes, where instead the focus is on mechanisms, institutions and actors that cause deprivation.

Sen considers that Economic capability (poverty), gender, age, caste and religion, *etc*., are important variables which indicate exclusion from social and economic opportunities. Amartya Sen (1999), has pointed out that the concept of social exclusion has to take into cognizance the issues regarding poverty and deprivation. According to Sen, poverty is the lack of capability to live a decent life as social beings and it has to be centre staged in any strategy on social exclusion. There is already evidence that poverty, social exclusion and deprivation have a major impact on health. Absolute poverty *i.e.*, lack of basic necessities for life still exists in many countries including developed countries and these sections are increasingly at risk including premature death. Relative poverty which excludes people from basic amenities such as housing, water, *etc.*, also leads to ill-health and premature deaths (Wilkinson and Marmot 1998). Especially women and children are affected by such deprivations.

REVIEW OF LITERATURE

Reproductive Health means more than bio-medical interventions. Reproductive Health affects, and is affected by, the broader context of people's lives – their economic circumstances, education, employment, living conditions, family environment, social and gender relationship, and the traditional and legal structures within which they live. It involves a greater awareness of health by individuals so that they can promote and protect their own reproductive health. It implies the involvement of other sectors, notably in education, finance and planning.

Reproductive Health in India is largely influenced by poverty-related and socio-culture factors on the one hand, and programme interventions on the other. Socio-cultural factors which impinge reproductive health include women's lack of awareness of health practices, strong seclusion norms which inhibit health-seeking, adolescent marriage, large family size norms which encourage frequent and closely spaced pregnancies, and a general devaluation of women which makes them the last to obtain food or health care and which requires of them long periods of physical activity.

Therefore, a brief review of literature relating to different aspects of reproductive health is presented in the following pages. More specifically the review is concerned with such aspects as age at marriage, age at birth, delivery practices, maternal health care, access and utilization of maternal health care services.

Marriage

Often times, the decision on what reproductive health status woman want, depends on their sexual partner, cultural orientation and often times their health care provider. (Noel L. Espallardo, 2004).

The proportion of women and men who are married young has important policy and programme implications. At the national level, 27 per cent of 15-19 year old women are currently married (15 per cent of urban women and 33 per cent of rural women) (NFHS-3, 2007).

More than one-quarter (27 per cent) of Indian women age 20-49 married before age 15; over half (58 per cent) married before the legal minimum marriage age of 18, and three-quarters (74 per cent) married before reaching age 20 (NFHS-3, 2007).

Following marriage, there are socio-cultural pressures on the young women to conceive as soon as possible. This is one means whereby she can attain both prestige & security in her new home. Hence, adolescent marriage is synonymous with adolescent child bearing. The efforts to increase in the median age at first marriage are proceeding at a very slow pace, and a considerable proportion of women still marry below the legal minimum age at marriage. The median age at first marriage among women age 20-49 is 17.2. More than one-quarter (27 per cent) of Indian women age 20-49 married before age 15; over half (58 per cent) married before the legal minimum marriage age of 18, and three-quarters (74 per cent) married before reaching age 20.(NFHS-3). One-fifth of the boys and a little more than one-fourth of the girls got married below the corresponding specified legal age for marriage. This proportion is much higher in the rural areas compared to urban areas of the country. (DLHS2002-04, 2006).

Notwithstanding these currents, NFHS-3 data indicates a promising trend for future. It reveals that over time, however, there has been a considerable increase in the median age at first marriage. The median age at first marriage in India is almost two years higher for women age 20-24 than for women age 45-49.

Social behaviour in the family environment is another important cause of sexual health problems especially among adolescents. Adolescents are at the cross-road between childhood and adulthood, hence their decision-making ability is not yet mature. They are not fully aware of available services and options. Lastly, they have to confront societal perception resulting into poor access to health services (Michels, 2000).

Child Bearing

Child bearing is an important event in the reproductive health and poses greatest risk to the women.

Women in South Asia have more pregnancies than in any other region of the world other than Sub-Saharan Africa.

Women in India remain largely valued for their reproductive performance and large numbers of children and sons in particular (at least two) are widely desired. With a total fertility rate of 4.3, the average woman spends a large proportion – about one-third – of her reproductive years in pregnancy and lactation.

Early, frequent and rapid child bearing is then the norm, reinforcing, in turn, women's already poor reproductive health and enhancing their chances of pregnancy related complications. High rates of maternal morbidity, mortality are associated with birth intervals conception during lactation period (Ramachandran, 1989; Sadik, 1980; Chatterjee, 1989; Royston and Armstrong, 1989) Unfortunately there are few studies in India on the relationship between birth intervals and maternal depletion, health or mortality.

The life time risk of dying from pregnancy related causes in India—with a total fertility rate of 4-5 and a maternal mortality ratio of around 500 per 10,000 live births – is as high as one in 27 (Royston and Armstrong, 1989). Maternal deaths in India account for about one per cent of all deaths and two per cent of all female deaths annually—but this translates into over ten per cent of all deaths among women in the reproductive ages and 13.2 per cent among rural women in 1987 (UNICEF, 1991).

There are very few community or household level studies of maternal mortality. Notable among these is a 1985-86 village level study in Anantapur, Andhra Pradesh (Bhatia, 1988). Unfortunately, maternal deaths are notoriously under-reported even in the more developed world, since often when the cause of death is a non-obstetric condition, precipitated by an obstetric condition, the latter is not reported; underestimates in the range of 33-50 per cent have thus been observed even in the USA (Royston and Armstrong, 1989).

The age at which women start child-bearing is an important demographic determinant of fertility. A higher median age at first birth is an indicator of lower fertility. The early onset of childbearing has disturbing consequences for reproductive health. It is estimated that as many as 10-15 per cent of all births annually occur to women in their early teens, before they are physically fully developed (Mathai, 1989; Kapil, 1990; Ramachandran, 1989; Leslie, 1991; Registrar General, 1987; rates for adolescents are not separately available). (Acsadi and Johnson-Acsadi, 1990).

The early onset of child-bearing has disturbing consequences for reproductive health. A common consequence of early marriage and childbearing is that girls enter marriage and become mothers without adequate information about reproductive and sexual heath issues, including sexual intercourse, contraception, sexually transmitted infections (STIs), pregnancy and childbirth (Mensch *et al.*, 1998; Singh and Samara, 1998). It is estimated that as many as 10-15 per cent of all births annually occur to women in their teens, before they are physically fully developed (Mathai, 1989; Kapil, 1990).

Because of social problems among adolescents, teenage pregnancy is an increasing problem in women's reproductive health. Teenage mothers and their children face poorer prospects in life than do women who delay motherhood until later in life. Early sexual intercourse, poor educational attainment, family background and interpersonal communication at home appear to be important factors that lead to increase probability of early pregnancy (Wellings, 1999).

According to NFHS-3 the median age at first birth for women among women age 20-49 years by current age according to caste for Scheduled Castes was 19.00 years and for other backward castes 19.6 years. Further the report reveals that five per cent of women age 25-49 have given birth by age 15. The percentage who gave births by age 15 decreases steadily from six per cent among women age 35-39 to one per cent among women aged 15-19. 30 per cent of women age 25-49 gave births before age 18 and 53 per cent gave births by age 20.

Among women aged 15-49 in India and are currently married the mean of children ever born and living is 2.85. The mean number of children ever bore increases steadily with age, reaching a high of 4.24 children for currently married women aged 45-49. Early child bearing is fairly common in India. 44 per cent of currently married women aged 15-19 years have already had a child (NFHS-3, 2007). On the average women who are completing reproductive period have given birth to four children in their reproductive life of which 3.5 children are surviving on the average (DLHS-2002-04, 2006).

Based on estimates for the three-year period before NFHS-3, the CBR was 23.1 births per 1,000 population and the TFR was 2.7 births per woman. The CBR is 25.0 in rural areas and 18.8 in urban areas, slightly lower than 2004 CBR estimates of 25.9 in rural areas and 19.0 in urban areas from the Sample Registration System (Office of the Registrar General, 2006b).

An inverse association between mean children ever born and educational attainment of women and also with the level of household economic comfort for the country as a whole was reported by the DLHS-RCH.

The family health surveys reveal encouraging trends of decreasing fertility in India. The decrease in fertility over time is evident from a comparison of the birth-order distribution in 1998 to 2005 (the tree rounds of NFHS-1, NFHS-2, and NFHS-3) for ever-married women. The proportion of births of order, four or higher decreased from 31 per cent in 1998 (NFHS-1, 1992-93) to 28 per cent in NFHS-2 and 25 per cent in 2005 (NFHS-3).

Birth Order is found to be associated with caste and education differentials. The proportion of births of orders four or higher is particularly high for births to women with no education (41 per cent), and Scheduled Tribe women (35 per cent). The proportion births of order four or higher is only 3 per cent for women with 12 or more years of education (NFHS-3, 2007). The occurrence of births of the third order and above is more among women from Scheduled Tribe (49 per cent), than among women from Scheduled Caste (46 per cent), Other Backward Class (42 per cent) and other castes (35 per cent). (DLHS2002-04, 2006).

WHO reports and some professional organizations highlighted the problems of fragmentation and lack of continuity of reproductive health services specifically in antenatal care. Women's health care has been separated into organ systems with different physicians providing care. This results to gaps and redundancies in care (Clancy, 1992). Women have to consult more than two physicians for their medical problems (Weisman, 2000), making health seeking more complex and costly.

Maternal Health Care

About 34 per cent of the women experienced at least one pregnancy related problem. The proportion was slightly lower among rural women (34 per cent) than among urban women (36 per cent). The major problems reported were 'swelling of hand and feet' (20 per cent), 'paleness' (13 per cent), and 'visual disturbance' (8 per cent). Only two per cent reported 'abnormal position of foetus', and 'vaginal bleeding'. About four per cent of the women reported 'convulsions' and three per cent reported 'weak or no movement of foetus' (DLHS-2002-04, 2006).

The pregnancy-related health problems most commonly reported are excessive fatigue (48 per cent) and swelling of the legs, body, or face (25 per cent). Ten per cent of mothers had convulsions that were not from fever and nine per cent reported night blindness. Only four per cent had any vaginal bleeding. The reported prevalence of both kinds of vision problems, convulsions that were not from fever, and excessive fatigue is higher in rural than in urban areas. In contrast, swelling of the legs, body, or face is more prevalent in urban areas (NFHS-3, 2007).

Pregnancy Outcome

The National Population Policy (NPP) adopted by the Government of India in 2000 (Ministry of Health and Family Welfare, 2000); reiterates the Government's commitment to the safe motherhood programme within the wider context of reproductive health. Among the national socio-demographic goals for 2010 specified by the policy, several goals pertain to safe motherhood, 80 per cent of all deliveries should take place in institutions by 2010, hundred per cent deliveries should be attended by trained personnel, and the maternal mortality ratio should be reduced to a level below 100 per 100,000 live births.

The literature however, suggests that for the most part, delivery continues to be conducted under unhygienic conditions. (Sharma and Bali, 1989; Kumar *et al*., 1988). Less than 40 per cent of births in India take place in health facilities. The majority of the institutional deliveries were conducted in private institutions (22 per cent of total deliveries) as against in government institution 19 per cent of total deliveries. A large proportion of the births (59 per cent) took place at home (NFHS-3, 2007).

NFHS-3 further observed that with regard to deliveries at home, the proportion of deliveries in a woman's own home increases and the proportion in her parents' home decreases with age and birth order. Mother's education and household wealth both have a strong negative association with deliveries at home.

Obstetric care from a trained provider during delivery is recognized as critical for the reduction of maternal and neonatal mortality. The delivery attended by skilled personnel is referred as safe deliveries.

Births delivered at home are more likely than births delivered in a health facility to be assisted by a health professional. Less than half of the births are safe in India.

In India, A large proportion of the births (59 per cent) take place at home. Only seven per cent of the total deliveries, that took place at home, were assisted by midwifery trained persons i.e. Doctor/Nurse and ANM. Forty-seven per cent of births were assisted by health personnel, including 35 per cent by a Doctor and 10 per cent by an ANM, Nurse, Midwife, or LHV. More than one-third of births (37 per cent) were assisted by a traditional birth attendant (TBA) and 16 per cent were assisted by only friends, relatives, or other persons. (DLHS-2002-04, 2006).

The proportion of safe deliveries decreases as parity rises 1 (66 per cent) to 4 and above (24 per cent). Only 28 per cent of births to women from Scheduled Tribes are safe, compared to 40 per cent among Scheduled Tribes, 48 per cent among Other Backward Classes, and 61 per cent of births among women from the 'other' castes category. The percentage of safe deliveries increased substantially with women's education and standard of living.

The percentage of births attended by a health professional decreases steadily with increasing parity women home deliveries are more likely to be attendant by health professionals among women with a high standard of living (27 per cent) than among women with lower and middle, SLI. Only eight per cent of births to Scheduled Tribes, 10 per cent to Scheduled Castes, 12 per cent to Other Backward Classes and 16 per cent births to women who belong to the 'other' caste category were attended by health professionals.

Traditionally, little attention has been paid to women in the antenatal period, even Traditional Dais coming into the picture only at delivery. The maternal and child health programme seeks to address this period of neglect. Under this programme, all pregnant women are to be routinely followed up either in the health centre or at home, and provided immunization, iron supplementation and regular check-ups to monitor the pregnancy. Women who have received antenatal care experience lower maternal and early infant mortality, fewer complication and higher birth weight (Bhatia, 1988; Mehta and Jayant, 1981; Mehta, 1989; Ares *et al*., 1990). As a result of limited contacts antenatela contacts, high-risk escape identification (Singh and Paul, 1988; Kapil, 1990).

Tetanus is held to account for anywhere between one-and-two-third of all neonatal death (Sokhy, 1988; Singh and Paul, 1988; UNICEF, 1984; Kapil, 1990; Agarwal and Agarwal, 1987). As a result of poor antenatal immunization, neonatal tetanus persists. (Sokhey, 1988; Singh and Paul, 1988, UNICEF, 1991).

There exists in India a wide range of cultural practices regarding diet during pregnancy, both on how much hand on what to eat. Unfortunately these are unlikely to foster improvements in antenatal nutrition (Ramchandran, 1989; Khan *et al.*, 1988; Tripathi *et al.*, 1987). As a result, anaemia is widespread among pregnant women (hemoglobin levels below 11 grams/dl); it is estimated to range from 40-50 per cent in urban areas to 50-70 per cent in rural areas (UNICEF, 1991; Kapil, 1990; Bhardwaj *et al.*, 1990; Mathai, 1989), higher in such states as Bihar and Utter Pradesh (Agarwal and Agarwal, 1987) and almost 90 per cent in rural area where hookworm infestation is endemic (Ramachandran, 1989; Srikantia, 1989a; Kapil, 1990). Consequences of maternal anaemia for infants are equally acute. (Ramachandran, 1989; Mathai, 1989; Ramalinga-swami, 1985; Singh, 1986).

Food and iron supplementation have been found to improve such maternal health attributes as weight gain, incidence of anaemia, complications during pregnancy and childbirth and birth weight (Dawn and Mitra, 1990; Iyengar, 1975).

The national anemia prophylaxis programme of iron and folic acid distribution, in which pregnant women are provided with 100 iron and folic acid tablets during pregnancy, was initiated as early as the 1950s. However, both service statistics and sample surveys confirm that this programme has not been very successful. From service statistics, were find that no more than an estimated one-third of all pregnant and lactating women (as estimated from population and birth rate figures for 1988 089) have received iron and folic acid supplementation (Ministry of

Welfare, Dept. of Women and Child Development, 1991; Jain and Agarwal, 1986). Even more discouraging are the results of the few sample surveys (Khan *et al.*, 1988). A micro-level evaluation by the Indian Council of Medical Research has shown that the programme has had little effect on the prevalence of anemia among pregnant women (UNICEF, 1991).

While antenatal care undoubtedly improves maternal and infant well-being, this service reaches few pregnant women.

On the national level, it is estimated that no more than 40-50 per cent of all regnant women in India receive any antenatal care at all (Singh and Paul, 1988; Stars and Measham, 1990; Acsadi and Johnos-Acsadi, 1990).

And fewer women are actually registered for antenatal care: only 21 per cent of all pregnant women in the rural sector and 47 per cent in the urban (UNICEF, 1991 quoting NSS, 1986-87). Local level sample surveys give a more disturbing picture of ANC service utilization and programme awareness (see also Gopalan, 1989; Mathai, 1989; Kanitkar and Sinha, 1989; Khan and Prasad, 1983; Mehta *et al.*, 1983; Khan *et al.*, 1988) and Punjab (Bhatinda District, Singh *et al.*, 1988). Where visits do occur, they occur infrequently and their content is unclear (Jain and Agarwal, 1986; Murthy *et al.*, 1990). (Whereas at least five antenatal check-ups are considered ideal, pregnant women who received antenatal care have rarely had more than one or two contacts and that too only when halfway through the pregnancy (Gopalan, 1989). The reasons for this poor utilization of services are cultural and socio-economic condition one hand and a result of poor quality of services on the other (Kanitakr and Sinha, 1989).

Six per cent of home deliveries to women who did not have any antenatal check-ups were attended by health professionals compared with 24 per cent of home deliveries to women who had four more antenatal check-ups. About 11 per cent home deliveries that were normal were attended by a health professional.

About 13 per cent of home deliveries attended by a health professional with availability of health facility in the village compared to 9 per cent non-availability of health facility in the village.

Access

The review of literature suggests that access to services has bearing on maternal health care and on reproductive health of women. For instance, Greene (2005), points out that currently there is much evidence to suggest that although access may be increasing at a national level in some countries, access is not equal across different social groups. Poverty is a key factor excluding many from accessing services. For example, studies have found that access to a skilled birth attendant at delivery is over three times higher for women in the richest quintile than those in the poorest in sub-Saharan Africa, and eight times higher in South Asia (Greene, 2005). Hemminki (1997), also noted that Access to care and the experience of treatment are also difficult among women in the lower socio-economic status (Hemminki, 1997). Similarly, Molesworth, K. (2005), observed that poor communications and transport infrastructure can be important in preventing access to services in rural areas, especially in maternal health care where transport to referral services is an essential component of dealing with emergencies and preventing mortality (Molesworth, 2005).

The low social status of women also limits their access to care when it is needed. In some cases, exclusion or because decision-making is the responsibility of other family members, women may not seek care for certain illnesses (Pang Ruyan, 2001). As a result there is poor quality health care, lack of access to Health care, work and environment neglect and hazards, and inefficiency of health care.

The lack of social support is often a hindrance for women seeking health care (Pitmann, 1999). Most women expressed distress over not being recognized as ill and cared for accordingly by family members, lack of companionship among friends and neighbours. Men on the other hand are encouraged by their wife and children to seek health care.

Access to care and the experience of treatment are also difficult among women in the lower socio-economic status (Hemminki, 1997).

Many studies have documented how traditional practices and beliefs also affect access to services. For example, in many countries it is standard practice to seek the services of traditional healers over public health service providers, in particular for SRH issues; a study in India found that many pregnant women preferred services of a lay attendant to those of a midwife (Matthews, 2005)

While poor quality of care can inhibit women from seeking health care, women's lack of autonomy in decision-making or movement is also an important constraint on women's health seeking. Women are, by and large, taught self-denial and modesty from an early age and are hence unlikely to acknowledge a health problem, and particularly a gynecological problem, unless it is very advance (SEWA-Rural, 1994). For example, large number of women experience white discharges but considers it as part of their lives and rarely seeks medical care for such a problem. Lack of decision-making, freedom of movement and time can restrict visits to health centres, even where a health problem has been recognized. Moreover, pelvic examinations are strongly resisted by women. And even if a problem has been diagnosed, treatment of it frequently not followed through because it is seen as an unnecessary expense or too demanding.

STATEMENT OF THE PROBLEM

Population health research has taught us that social and health inequality hurts *everyone*, not just those at the bottom. Similarly, *everyone* is hurt by social exclusion. Therefore, the key association between social inclusion and the social determinants is social and health inequities (Health Canada, 2001).

Research also shows that the causal direction from social inequities to social exclusion to health inequities is multi-directional and mutually reinforcing in feedback loops (World Health Organization, 2005). Decades of research have further shown that social exclusion impacts health and is aggravated by health status (World Health Organization, 2005).

Social exclusion and a lack of participation in decision-making arising from deficits in the Social Determinants of Health (SDOH) are major contributors to premature morbidity and death (Wilkinson and Marmot, 1998).

The consequences of social exclusion are manifested through social fragmentation and the loss of social cohesion resulting in state dependency, family breakdown, homelessness, criminality and substance abuse (Bynner, 1998), as well as institutional problems in education, health, nourishment, crime, violence, social divisions, racism and xenophobia (Klasen, 1998).

Gender, health and poverty are strongly inter-connected and there is a strong rural dimension but according to WHO, the appropriate detailed studies and data collection of rural women's health circumstances have not been undertaken. Maternal health care and infant mortality statistics need to be collected and examined in relation to social exclusion and the level of rural infrastructural services present. Accessibility in respect of women's special health needs associated with their reproductive function needs to be undertaken: identification of the gender and household resource constraints, such as taboos and cultural customs, which prevent women accessing health facilities or place women in specific health danger in any particular location needs to be undertaken and a comprehensive data mapping of such patterns needs to be developed. As women have particular health needs examining the proportion of access to reproductive health will provide an early indicator as to whether women have been adequately included or participate in rural health services.

Reproductive Health in India is largely influenced by poverty-related and socio-culture factors on the one hand, and programme interventions on the other. Socio-cultural factors which impinge reproductive health include women's lack of awareness of health practices, strong seclusion norms which inhibit health-seeking, adolescent marriage, large family size norms which encourage frequent and closely spaced pregnancies, and a general devaluation of women which makes them the last to obtain food or health care and which requires of them long periods of physical activity.

To overcome social exclusion in the area of health, India adopted the development approach. In the development approach, improvement in health status is viewed primarily as a product of socio-economic development. By definition, development implies improved nutrition, hygienic living and working conditions, greater awareness of health problems and wider accessibility to health care services which have a favourable effect on the health status of the people. Improvements in health status as well as health care are treated as integrated components of the development process, in which medical care is just one of the many inputs; the impact of state intervention on health status depends on its overall socio-economic policies.

Accordingly, India during the past few decades made a bold and impressive, determined and planned effort to empower health status of its populace. Over the years it has adopted a two faced strategy to usher social inclusion. On one hand it strived to achieve overall socio-economic development with equity to influence and enhance the health status; and on the other it has attempted to raise the health status independent of socio-economic development through state intervention by extending health care with equity. RCH was one such programme which was launched in the year 1997.

The available literature is inadequate when it comes to assessing reproductive health and its underlying causes. Rigorous indirect estimates of maternal mortality, at the state and district levels are essential. Micro-level analyses of the links between reproductive health outcomes and their socio-economic and cultural antecedents in different settings would go a long way in tailoring services in locally relevant way. So, studies on the impact of interventions designed to redress reproductive health deficiencies.

In view of the above reflections an attempt is made in this study to study **the practices of social exclusion and achievements of social inclusion** of reproductive health practices of a backward, indigenous and traditional communities in a chronically drought prone and backward district.

The present study is focused on women and is undertaken in the context of selected indigenous and traditional communities. These communities are spread in the remote and backward pockets of a backward district namely Anantapur District, Andhra Pradesh. The habitations are border to the Karnataka State.

AIMS AND OBJECTIVES

The present study aims at understanding the **social exclusion and social inclusion of reproductive health practices of a backward, indigenous and traditional communities**. The following objectives are framed to determine the scope of the study and to facilitate a scientific study.

The study objectives are:

a. To portray the socio-economic characteristics of selected **backward, indigenous and traditional communities;**

b. To analyze the access to communication, education & health services and facilities to the selected communities;

c. To examine the reproductive health status of the selected communities;

d. To analyze the reproductive health practices of the selected communities;

e. To obtain data on the indicators of reproductive health; and

f. To examine the practice of Social Exclusion and Social Inclusion in relation to the reproductive health care and practices of the communities under reference.

METHOD OF STUDY

Universe

The Universe of the study is Anantapur District of Andhra Pradesh. Anantapur District is located in a **rain**

shadow region and is a chronically drought prone backward district. It enjoys the dubious distinction of receiving second lowest rainfall in the country. It's a multi-caste district with higher concentration of Backward Castes, De-notified Nomadic Tribes and Scheduled Cates.

The district is divided into 63 revenue mandals and comprises (3322) habitations/villages.

The selected communities for the present study are Boya (De-notified Nomadic Tribe), Adavi Golla Community (a Backward Class Community) and Madiga Community (Scheduled Caste Community). These communities are numerically larger than the other communities in the district. The selected communities are considered to be socio-culturally marginalized and vulnerable communities being poor and continue to hold archaic beliefs and practices.

Sampling

For the purpose of study an attempt is made to elicit information with regard to the spread of the communities in the various revenue mandals from different sources such as caste associations/bodies, Zilla Parishad officials, Revenue officials and Health officials. Our information is that though Boya and Madiga communities are widely spread in all most all the revenue mandals, the Adavi Gollas are however, are confined to only a few mandals.

Therefore, in the present study *Multi-stage Random Sampling* technique was adopted to draw the study sample. The stages involved are selection of mandals, selection of villages and the selection of households. In the process of sample selection the following criteria were kept in mind:

- Female literacy;
- Presence and numerical spread of the selected communities in the mandals.

Based on the above criteria, at **the first stage** five revenue mandals out of 63 revenue mandals in the district were considered. These are Amarapuram, Agali, Gudibanda, Madakasira and Rolla Revenue Mandals.

At the **second stage** nineteen villages for the selected revenue mandals were selected. At **third stage** 10 per cent of households from each of the selected communities from each of the selected villages were randomly selected. The details of the sampling frame are presented in the Table 1.1.

Table 1.1: The Details of the Sampling Frame.

No. of Revenue Mandals	No. of Mandals Selected	No. Villages in the Selected Mandals	No. of Villages Selected	Total No. of households in the Selected Villages	No. of households Selected
63	5	267	19	3766	229

Thus our study sample comprise 229 households represent Boya (60), Adavigolla (100) and Madiga communities (63).

Tools of Data Collection

The present study is based on empirical data. For the purpose of primary data collection tools like interview schedule and Focus groups discussion are considered.

The interview schedule is designed to elicit the data on the following broad areas:

- ❑ Socio-economic Data,
- ❑ Family Background,
- ❑ Facilities and Amenities,

- Reproductive Health Status,
- Reproductive Health Care,
- Reproductive Health practices and reproductive track infections,
- Utilization of Health Services.

Table 1.2: Study Villages.

Name of the selected Mandal	Name of the selected Village	No. of selected Households
Agali	Reddiganapalli H.D. Halli	11 10
Gudibanda	Pharam Rallapalli P.G. Hatti Mynagan Pally Keynchayyana	10 19 10 11 8
Rolla	Rolla Kallurappam Galla Rolla Golla Hatti	31 10 10
Madakasira	A. Golla Hatti E. Golla Hatti Chipuleti Gondanahalli Jammam Palli Vadra Palyam	10 10 10 10 10 10
Amarapuram	Valasa Thammadapalla Gollamarana Hatti	10 19 10
		229

The focused group discussions are held to gather information on the archaic practices related to reproductive health.

In addition to the primary data, secondary data from the official records/publications were collected.

Data Collection

Data will be collected in three stages. At the first stage preliminary information regarding the villages under reference will be collected. The pre-testing of the interview schedule also will be carried out.

At the second stage several focus group discussions will be held in all the nineteen selected villages. The focus group discussions will be held separately with each of the selected communities. The purpose of focus group discussion is to establish rapport with the selected communities in addition to the primary purpose of collecting information with regard to archaic practices related to reproductive health practices.

The third stage data will be collected through house hold survey of selected communities by administering interview schedule.

Data Analysis

The primary data will be analyzed by processing through computer. The standard SPSS package will be used for data analysis. The independent variables considered for the purpose of analysis are Caste, Age. The dependent variables considered are Reproductive health status indicators, Reproductive health care indicators, the reproductive health practice indicators and R.T.I., indicators.

Wherever necessary the statistical tools like percentages, ratios, averages were employed.

SCHEME OF PRESENTATION

The present study is presented in six chapters.

The **first** chapter provides introduction to the study, the review of literature, the issues under study and the method of study.

The **second** chapter presents Reproductive Health Practices and the status of reproductive health in India.

Third chapter explains health infrastructure, health care service in India.

The **fourth** chapter presents the profile of the Anantapur District and the socio-economic profile of the respondents.

The **fifth** chapter presents the analysis and discussions of the study.

The **sixth** chapter presents the summary and conclusions of the study.

REFERENCES

1. Acsadi, George T.F. and Gwendolyn Johnson-Acsadi. 1990. "Safe motherhood in South Asia socio-cultural and demographic aspects of maternal health", Background Paper, Safe Motherhood South Asia Conference, Lahore.
2. Agarwal, D.K. and K.N. Agarwal. 1987. 'Early childhood mortality in Bihar and Uttar Pradesh', Indian Pediatrics 24, No.8 (August), 627-32.
3. Aras, R., N. Pai, and A. Purandare, 1990. 'Perinatal mortality – a retrospective hospital study', Journal of Obstetrics and Gynaecology 40, No.3 (June): 365-69.
4. Berger, J. 2004. 'Re-sexualizing the epidemic: Desire, risk and HIV prevention', Development Update, 5(3), 45-67, Johannesburg.
5. Bhardwaj, N. *et al.*, 1990. 'Socio-economic factors affecting weight gain in pregnancy', Journal of Obstetrics and Gynaecology 40, No.3 (June): 327-30.

6. Bhatia, J.C. 1988. 'A Study of Maternal Mortality in Anantapur District, Andhra Pradesh, India', Bangalore: Indian Institute of Management.

7. Bynner, John. 1998. 'Use of Longitudinal Data in the Study of Social Exclusion. OECD: Centre for Educational Research and Innovation. [http://www.oecd.org/els/edu/ceri/conf220299.htm].

8. Chatterjee, Meera. 1989. 'Socio-economic and socio-cultural influences on women's nutritional status roles' in C. Gopalan and Suminer Kaur (eds), Women and Nutrition in India, New Delhi: Nutrition Foundation of India.

9. Clancy C. and Massion C. 1992. 'American women's health care: a patchwork quilt with gaps', JAMA, 268: 1918-1920.

10. Dawn, C.S. and Bani Kumar Mitra. 1990. 'Effect of food supplementation on maternal weight gain, low birth weight incidence, infant weight gain and btreast feed performance', Journal of Obstetrics and Gynaecology 40, No.3 (June): 313-18.

11. District Level Health Survey (DLHS-2, 2002-04). 2006. 'Reproductive and Child Health', International Institute of Population Sciences (Deemed University), Mumbai.

12. Gopalan, C. 1989. 'Women and Nutrition in India–general consideration', in C. Gopalan and Suminder Kaur (eds), Women and Nutrition in India, New Delhi: Nutrition Foundation of India.

13. Green ME & Merrick T, 2005. 'Poverty Reduction: Does reproductive health matter?', HNP discussion paper, World Bank, Washington DC.

14. Health Canada, 2001. 'Social Capital, Social Cohesion, Social Inclusion/Exclusion', Population Health Newsletter, Ottawa.

15. Hemminki E., Sihvo S., Koponen P. and Kosumen E. 1997. 'Quality of contraceptive services in Finland', Qual Health Care, 6:62-68.

16. Iyengar, L. 1975. 'Influence of the diet on the outcome of pregnancy in Indian women', in Proceedings of the 9th International Congress of Nutrition, Mexico, 1972, Vol. 2, Karger, Nutrition, pp.48-53.

17. Jain, M.L. and Dinesh Agarwal. 1986. 'Utilization of maternal services in an ICDS BLOCK', Journal of Obstetrics and Gynaecology 36, N.5 (October): 842-44.

18. Jo Beall and Laure-Hélène Piron. 2005. 'DFID Social Exclusion Review', The London School of Economics and Political Science.

19. Kanitkar, Tara and R.K. Sinha, 1989. 'Antenatal care services in five states of India'. In S.N. Singh, M.K. Premi, P.S./ Bhatia and Ashish Bose (eds.), Population Transition in India, Vol. 2, pp.201-11, Delhi: B.R. Publishing Corporation.

20. Kapil, U., 1990. 'Promotion of safe motherhood in India,' Indian Pediatrics, 27: No.3 (March): pp. 232-238.

21. Khan, M.E. and C.V.S. Prasad, 1983. 'Under-utilization of health services in rural India: A comparative study of Bihar, Gujarat and Kerala, Baroda', Operations Research Group.

22. Khan, M.E., Richard Anker, S.K. Ghosh Dastidar and Sashi Airathi. 1988. 'Inequalities between men and women in nutrition and family welfare services: an in-dept equiry in an Indian Village', Social Action 38 (October-December).

23. Klasen, Stephan. 1998. 'Social Exclusion and Children in OECD Countries: Some Conceptual Issue'. OECD: Centre for Educational Research and Innovation. [http://www.oecd.org/els/edu/ceri/conf220299.htm].

24. Kumar, Harsh, S. Aneja, V.K. Prasad, S.K. Arora and D.N. Mulick. 1988. 'Tetanus neonatorum: Clinico-epidemiologicla profile', Indian Pediatrics 25, No.11 (November): 1054-1057.

25. Lieslie, Joanne., 1991. 'Women's Nutrition: the key to improving health in developing countries', Health Policy and Planning, No.1, pp.1-19.

26. Mathai, Sharmma, T. 1989. 'Women and the Health System' in C. Gopalan and Suminder Kaur (Eds.), Women and Nutrition in India, New Delhi, Nutrition Foundation of India.

27. Matthews Z., Ramakrishna J., Mahendra S., Kilaru A., Ganapathy S. 2005. 'Birth rights and rituals in rural south India: care seeking in the intrapartum period," Journal of Bio-social Science, 37(4), 385-411.

28. Mehta, A. and K. Jayant. 1981. 'Parinatal Mortality Survey in India (1977-79), Part I, Identification of health intervention needs', Journal of Obstetric Gynaecology 32, No.2 (April): 183-215.

29. Mehta, A. M.E. Khan, R.B. Gupta, M.M. Gandotra and O.S. Ojha. 1983. 'Role of Health Services Delivery on Acceptance of Family Planning, New Delhi: ICMR, Mimeo.

30. Mensch, B., J. Bruce and B. Greene. 1998. 'The Uncharted Passage: Girls' Adolescents in the Developing World, Population Council, New York.

31. Michels T. 2000. "Patients like us": Pregnant and parenting teens

view the health care system., Public Health Rep., 115: 557-575.

32. Ministry of Welfare, Dept. of Women and Child Development, 1991. '15th year of ICDS, an overview, New Delhi: Government of India.

33. Molesworth, K. 2005. 'The impact of transport provision on direct and proximate determinants of access to health services', Swiss Tropical Institute.

34. Murphy EM, Greene ME, Mihailovic A., Olupot-Olupot P. 2006. 'Was the "ABC" approach (abstinence, being faithful, using condoms) responsible for Uganda's decline in HIV?', PLoS Med 3(9): e379. DOI: 10.1371/journal.pmed.0030379.

35. Murthy, G.V., Anil Goswami and Saroja Narayanan. 1990. 'Utilization patterns of antenatal services in an urban slum', Journal Obestetrics and Gynaecology 40, No.1 (February): 42-46.

36. National Family Health Survey of India (NFHS-3). 2007. International Institute of Population Sciences (Deemed University), Mumbai.

37. National Family Health Survey of India (NHFS-1), 1992-93. International Institute for Population Sciences (Deemed University), Bombay.

38. National Family Health Survey of India (NHFS-2), 1998-99. International Institute for Population Sciences (Deemed University), Bombay.

39. Nayar, K.R. 2007. 'Social exclusion, caste & health: A review based on the social determinants framework' Indian J. Med. Res. 126, October, pp 355-363

40. Pang Ruyan. 2001. "The important issues in developing a national plan on maternal mortality. Department of Reproductive Health and Research." WHO, 2001.

41. Pittman. 1999. 'Gendered experiences for health care' Int. J. Qual Health Care, 11:397-405.

42. Ramachandran, Prema., 1989. 'Lactation-nutrition-fertility interaction', in C. Gopalan and Sluminder Kaur (Eds.), Women and Nutrition in India, New Delhi, Nutrition Foundation of India.

43. Ramalinga Swami, V. 1985. 'The state of life: Report of the National Seminar on reducing incidence of low birth weight babies in India, New Delhi: National Institute of Public Cooperation and Child Development.

44. Register General, 1987. 'Survey of causes of deaths (rural): annual report, 1984 and 1986', A Report, Series 3, No.17 and 19, New Delhi.

45. Royston, Eric and Sue Armstrong. 1989. 'Preventing Maternal Deaths', Geneva: World Health Organization.

46. Sadik, Jafis, 1980. 'Family Planning: Improving the Health of Women', Draper Fund Report, 9 (October).

47. Sen A. 1999. 'Development as Freedom', New Delhi: Oxford University Press.

48. Sharma, N. and P. Bali. 1989. 'A comparative study of maternal mortality and morbidity in a teaching hospital of Northern India', Journal of Obstetric and Gynecology, 38, No.2, p.177-181.

49. Singh Meharban. And V.K. Paul. 1988. 'Strategies to reduce perinatal and neonatal mortality', Indian ediatrics 23, No.6 (June): 499-509.

50. Singh, Meharban. 1986. 'Hospital based data on perinatal and neonatal mortality in India,' Indian Pediatrics 23, No.8 (August): 579-584.

51. Singh, Surinder, Jagieet Singh, Sushila Mittal, R.K.D. Goel, Tejbir Singh and S.K. Oberoi. 1988. 'A study of antenatal services in rural areas of district of Bathinda of Punjab', Journal of Obsetrics and Gynaecology 38, No.1 (February): 2-26.

52. Sokhy, J. 1988. 'Magnitude of problems in India', in Ministry of Health and Family Welfare, The Control of Neonatal Tetanus in India, pp. 16-23, New Delhi, Government of India, quoted in Singh and Paul.

53. Srikantia, S.G. 1989a. 'Nutritional deficiency diseases', in C. Gopalan and Suminder Kaur (eds.), Women and Nutrition in India, New Delhi: Nutrition Foundation of India.

54. Starrs, Ann and Diane Measham. 1990. "Challenge for the Nineties: Safe Motherhood in South Asia, New York and Washington: The World Bank and Family Care International.

55. Tripathi, A.M. D.K. Agarwarl, K.N. Agarwal, R.R. Devi and S. Cherian. 1987. 'Nutritional status of rural pregnant women and foetal outcome', Indian Pediatrics 24, No.9 (September): 703-712.

56. UNICEF, India. 1984, 'An analysis of the situation of children in India,' New Delhi.

57. UNICEF, India. 1991, 'Children and Women in India: a situation analysis,' New Delhi, UNICEF.

58. Weisman., 2000. 'The trends in health care delivery for women: Challenge for medical education,' Acad. Med., 75: 1107-1113.

59. Wellings K., Wadsworth J., Johnson A., Field J., Macdowall W., 'Teenage fertility and life chances Teenage fertility and life chances', Rev. Reprod, 1999 Sep., 4(3):184-90.

60. Wilkinson, R. and Marmot, M. 1998. 'Social Determinants of Health: The Solid Facts', World Health Organization, Copenhagen.

61. World Health Organization (WHO), 1994. 'Health, Population and Development', WHO Position Paper for the International Conference on Population and Development, Cairl, WHO/FHE/ 94.I, Geneva.

62. World Health Organization. 2005. 'Knowledge Network on Social Exclusion. Commission on the Social Determinants of Health Regional Consultation. Presentation. www.who.int/social-determinants.

63. Zurayk, H.H. *et al.*, 1993. 'Concepts and Measures of Reproductive Morbidity, Health Transition Review, 3(1):17-39.

CHAPTER 2 Reproductive Health Status in India

A Reproductive Health focus provides a means for addressing health and population issues with an emphasis on needs of women and men. Specific reproductive events, notably pregnancy and child bearing have an impact on women's health as well as on traditionally emphasized demographic trends. However, Reproductive Health presents a life long process inextricably linked to the status and role of women in their homes and societies and is not just related to the biological events of conception and birth.

Reproductive Health is defined as 'the ability of women to live through the reproductive years and beyond, with reproductive choice, dignity and successful child bearing, and to be free from gynecological diseases and risks'. Within the framework of WHOs definition of health as "a state of complete physical, mental and social well-being and not merely the absence of disease or infirmity, reproductive health addresses the reproductive processes, functions and systems at all stages of life.

Reproductive Health implies that people are able to have a responsible, satisfying and safe sex life, and that they have the capacity to reproduce and the freedom to decide if, when and how often, to do so. Implicit in this last condition are the right of men and women to be informed of and to have access to safe, effective, affordable and acceptable method of fertility regulation, of their choice, and the right of access to appropriate health services, that will enable women to go safely through their pregnancy and child birth and to provide couples with the best chance of having a healthy infant (WHO, 1994).

In the present chapter an attempt is made to sketch the Status of Reproductive Health of Women in India. For this purpose the secondary data derived from DLHS[1] and NFHS[2] are used. The status of reproductive health is portrayed with reference to such broad parameters as marriage, childbearing, delivery of child, health care during pregnancy and the knowledge about reproductive tract infections.

MARRIAGE

Marriage in India marks the point in a woman's life when childbearing becomes socially acceptable. Thus, Marriage in the household is an important event. Marriage is a principal indicator of women's exposure to the risk of pregnancy. Early age at marriage in a population is usually associated with a longer period of exposure to the risk of pregnancy and higher fertility levels.

Current Marital Status

In India seventy-five per cent of Indian women age 15-49 are currently married, less than 1 per cent are married but *gauna*[3] has not been performed, 3 per cent are widowed, and 1 per cent are divorced, separated, or deserted. One-fifth of Indian women age 15-49 have never been married (NHFS-3, 2007). The DLHS 2002-04 presents more details in this regard. The report reveals:

Twenty four per cent of females in the age group 15-19 years followed by 70 per cent in the age group 20-24 years, 90 per cent in the age group 25-29 years, 91 per cent in the age group 30-44 years, 76 per cent in the age group 45-59 years and 39 per cent of those 60 years and above are currently married.

The proportion of never married is 33 per cent in India, and it is higher for males (39 per cent) than for females (27 per cent). The proportion of never married among males declines with increasing age and it is one per cent never married by the time they are in the age group 45-59 years. A similar pattern has been observed in the case of females with the lowest never married proportion in the age group 60 years and above. The proportion of divorced, separated or widowed is negligible and concentrated to the older age group for both males and females. Sixty per cent of the women aged 60 years or older are widowed/divorced/separated. Among the de facto population aged 10 years and above, 57 per cent of males and 60 per cent of females are currently married.

Age at Marriage

Age at first marriage has a profound impact on childbearing (and this on reproductive health) because women who marry early have on average a longer period of exposure to pregnancy and a greater number of lifetime births. The minimum legal age at marriage in India is 21 years for males and 18 years for females. However, traditionally, early marriages are more common in India.

Increase in the median age at first marriage are proceeding at a very slow pace, and a considerable proportion of women still marry below the legal minimum age at marriage. One-fifth of the boys and a little more than one fourth of the girls got married below the corresponding specified legal age for marriage. This proportion is much higher in the rural areas compared to urban areas of the country. It is also found that, the percentage of girls who were married below the legal age for marriage is the highest in Bihar (52 per cent) and Rajasthan (49 per cent) and the lowest in Himachal Pradesh (13 per cent). (DLHS 2002-04, 2006). The median age at first marriage among women age 20-49 is 17.2. More than one-quarter (27 per cent) of Indian women age 20-49 married before age 15; over half (58 per cent) married before the legal minimum marriage age of 18, and three-quarters (74 per cent) married before reaching age 20. (NFHS-3, 2007).

But there has been steady rise in age at marriage. Not withstanding these currents, NFHS-3 data indicates a promising trend for future. It reveals that over time, however, there has been a considerable increase in the median age at first marriage. The median age at first marriage in India is almost two years higher for women age 20-24 than for women age 45-49. NFHS-3 report reveals that there is a gradual decline in the proportion of women married by ages 15, 18, and 20 years from the oldest to the youngest age groups. A particularly notable decline is seen in the proportions married by age 15 in the three youngest age groups, from 25 per cent of women age 25-29 to 12 per cent of women age 15-19.

This trend is supported by DLHS data too which shows that the mean age at marriage among the boys and girls in the country as 24.5 and 19.5 years respectively. Mean age at marriage for boys and girls in urban India are 26 years and 21 years respectively. The corresponding figures in rural areas are 24 years and 19 years respectively. The average age at marriage being 25 years for boys and 20 years for girls at the national level, both boys and girls oblige the legal age of marriage.

CHILD-BEARING

Child-bearing is an important event in the reproductive health and poses greatest risk to the women.

Women in South Asia have more pregnancies than in any other region of the world other than Sub-Saharan Africa. Women in India remain largely valued for their reproductive performance and large numbers of children and sons in particular (at least two) are widely desired. With a total fertility rate of 4.3, the average woman spends a large proportion – about one-third – of her reproductive years in pregnancy and lactation. Early, frequent and rapid child bearing is then the norm, reinforcing, in turn, women's already poor reproductive health and enhancing their chances of pregnancy related complications. Unfortunately there are few studies in India on the relationship between birth intervals and maternal depletion, health or mortality. An analysis of all maternal deaths occurring in three hospitals in Bangkok, however, confirms that women with a previous birth intervals of less than two years had a 250 per cent high risk of dying than women with a a longer birth interval (Royston and Armstrong, 1989). Studies in India (Ramachandran, 1989) indicate that morbidity among women who conceive during lactation is considerably higher than in other women; the mean birth weight of infants born within a twelve-month interval from a previous birth was significantly lower than those born after a twelve-month interval.

Finally, there is the familiar link between the length of the birth interval and infant mortality: a study in Punjab in the 1970s reports infant mortality rates of 206 for those born after an interval of less than one year, compared to 132 and 108 for births occurring after interval 2-3 and more than 4 years respectively (Sadik, 1980). Another study (Chatterjee, 1989) indicates that births occurring within 12 months of a previous one are exposed to a mortality rate of 200 compared to 100 in case where the birth interval exceeds 12 months. Apart from higher mortality, short birth intervals are associated with growth faltering of the immediately older sibling.

The process of childbearing can be best understood with reference to age at first birth, fertility of the women (children ever born and living), birth order, pregnancy outcome and pregnancy problems.

Age at First Birth

The age at which women start childbearing is an important demographic determinant of fertility. A higher median age at first birth is an indicator of lower fertility. Early childbearing is fairly common in India. Twelve per cent of all women age 15-19 and 44 per cent of currently married women aged 15-19 have already had a child. This trend of birth deliveries at younger ages in India is steadily decreasing. The same pattern of decreases at younger ages is evident for every exact age at birth.

Five per cent of women age 25-49 have given birth by age 15. The percentage who gave birth by age 15 decreases steadily from 6 per cent among women age 35-39 to 1 per cent among women age 15-19.

Thirty per cent of women age 25-49 gave birth before age 18 and 53 per cent gave birth by age 20. By age 25, 85 per cent of women age 25-49 have given birth. The median age at first birth is 20 for women age 20-49 in the country as a whole.

Age at first birth in India is found to be influenced by such factors as caste, education and standard of living/ wealth. The median age at first birth is six years higher for women who have completed 12 and more years of schooling than for women with no education.

By caste/tribe, women from other backward classes have a median age at first birth that is about half a year higher than that of women from scheduled castes or scheduled tribes, and women belonging to none of these groups have the highest median (20.6 years).

The median age at first birth increases steadily with wealth index quintiles. The median is more than three years higher for women in households in the highest wealth quintile than for women in households in the lowest wealth quintile.

Children ever Born and Living

A look at the mean children ever born by current age of women reveals that older women had experienced more average live births than younger women. Women with longer marital duration have higher mean children ever born. On the average, women who are married for 15 or more years have 3.9 children ever born and on the average 3.4 of them are surviving.

Among women age 15-49 in India, the mean number of children ever born is 2.26 for all women irrespective of marital status and 2.85 for currently married women. The mean number of children ever born increases steadily with age, reaching a high of 4.1 children for all women age 45-49 and 4.24 children for currently married women age 45-49.

On the average, women who are completing the reproductive period have given birth to 4 children in their reproductive life of which 3.5 children are surviving on the average.

Seventy per cent of urban total fertility and 63 per cent of rural total fertility are concentrated in the prime childbearing ages 20-29. Fertility at age 15-19 accounts for 14 per cent of total fertility in urban areas and 18 per cent in rural areas. Fertility at ages 35 and older accounts for only 4 per cent of total fertility in urban areas and 7 per cent in rural areas

Completed fertility in India varies from a low of 2.5 mean children ever born for Tripura and Kerala to the highest of 5.4 children in Uttar Pradesh. Completed fertility in terms of mean children ever born are high in the State/ Union Territory of Uttar Pradesh (5.4), Bihar (5.2), Nagaland, Meghalaya, Madhya Pradesh, and Rajasthan (4.7 each), Jharkhand (4.5), Arunachal Pradesh and Uttaranchal (4.3 each), Lakshadweep (4.0). With the exception of Tripura, Kerala, Goa, Tamil Nadu, Andaman and Nicobar Islands, Chandigarh and Pondicherry, mean children ever born in all States/Union Territories of India is more than 3 children. It is also true that in most of the States/Union Territories the mean number of male children is more than the mean of female children born to women in 40-44 years.

There is a clear rural-urban divide in terms of mean children ever born with 2.8 children in rural areas and 2.4 children in urban areas.

The average children ever born also vary by caste/tribe of the eligible women. For women belonging to scheduled caste and tribe, the mean children ever born are 2.9 each, other backward class is 2.7 and other caste is 2.5. By caste/tribe, the TFR is 0.6 children higher for scheduled caste women, 0.8 children higher for scheduled tribe women, and 0.4 children higher for women belonging to other backward classes (OBC) than for women who do not belong to any of these groups.

The mean children ever born is higher for non-literate women (3.3) than for women who have completed 0-9 years of schooling (2.3) and 10 or more years of schooling (1.7). The mean number of surviving children for women corresponding to these educational levels is 2.8, 2.2 and 1.7 respectively. The TFR for India is 1.8 children higher for women with no education than for women with 12 or more years of education.

For the country as a whole, the DLHS-RCH shows an inverse association between mean children ever born and educational attainment of women and also with the level of household economic comfort.

Further the mean children ever born for women classified into low, medium and high standard of living by SLI are 3.1, 2.6 and 2.2 respectively.

Birth Order

The distribution of births by birth order is yet another way to understand fertility.

Overall, the proportion of births at each order is larger than the proportion at the next higher order. Thirty-one per cent of all births are first-order births, 28 per cent are second-order births, 16 per cent are third-order births, and 25 per cent are births of order four or higher.

Seventy-seven per cent of births to mothers age 15-19 are of order one; by contrast, 65 per cent of births to mothers age 30-39 are of order four or higher. The proportion of births that are of order four or higher is 16 per cent in urban areas and 28 per cent in rural areas

By current age of eligible women, more than eighty per cent of births to women in the age group 35-39 years and 40-44 years are the fourth and higher order births. For women in the age group 15-19 years, 76 per cent of births are first order and 21 per cent of births are second order.

In the case of eligible women in urban areas 32 per cent of the births are of the third and higher order whereas births of these orders constitute 46 per cent for rural women indicating that higher order births are more concentrated in rural areas.

In India, births to non-literate women are of higher order whereas lower order births occurred to women who completed 10 or more years of schooling. The data from both the national surveys reveal this.

The proportion of births of order four or higher is particularly high for births to women with no education (41 per cent), and scheduled-tribe women (35 per cent). The proportion births of order four or higher is only 3 per cent for women with 12 or more years of education (NFHS-3, 2007).

Of the total births, to non-literate women, 57 per cent are third and higher order births, followed by 32 per cent for women with 0-9 years of schooling and 16 per cent for women who had 10 or more years of schooling.

The occurrence of births of the third order and above is more among women from scheduled tribe (49 per cent) than among women from scheduled caste (46 per cent), other backward class (42 per cent) and other castes (35 per cent). (DLHS - 2002-04, 2006).

Incidence of births of the third order and above for women classified by household standard of living index are 23 per cent for high, 36 per cent for medium and 52 per cent for low living standard household women.

The data on regional differentials in the third and higher birth order show clear division between the southern states that fall on the lower side and the Empowerment Action Group (EAG) states and some north-eastern states that fall on the higher end.

Third and higher order births form about 57 per cent of all births in Uttar Pradesh and Nagaland. The highest percentage is about 60 per cent in the state of Meghalaya and the lowest is about 16 per cent in Kerala.

Forty-two per cent of births to women in households in the lowest wealth quintile were of order four or higher, compared with just 6 per cent of births to women in households in the highest wealth quintile. The decrease in fertility over time is evident from a comparison of the birth-order distribution in 1998 to 2005 (the tree rounds of NFHS-1, NFHS-2, and NFHS-3) for ever-married women. The proportion of births of order four or higher decreased from 31 per cent in 1998 (NFHS-1) to 28 per cent in NFHS-2 and 25 per cent in 2005 (NFHS-3, 2007).

Health Problems during Pregnancy

Complications during pregnancy may affect both women's health and the outcome of the pregnancy adversely. Early detection of complications during pregnancy and their management are important components of the safe motherhood programme.

The following are a few pregnancy-related problems such as swelling of hands and feet, paleness, weak or no movement of foetus, abnormal position of foetus, difficulty with vision during daylight, night blindness, convulsions (not from fever), swelling of the legs, body or face, excessive fatigue, or vaginal bleeding and other problems.

Night blindness, or difficulty in seeing at dusk, is the result of chronic vitamin A deficiency and is often seen in pregnant women in areas where vitamin A deficiency is endemic. Convulsions accompanied by signs of hypertension can be symptomatic of eclampsia, a potentially fatal condition. The potential health risk posed by vaginal bleeding during pregnancy varies by when in the pregnancy the bleeding takes place.

The pregnancy-related health problems most commonly reported are excessive fatigue (48 per cent) and swelling of the legs, body, or face (25 per cent). Ten per cent of mothers had convulsions that were not from fever and 9 per cent reported night blindness. Only 4 per cent had any vaginal bleeding. The reported prevalence of both kinds of vision problems, convulsions that were not from fever, and excessive fatigue is higher in rural than in urban areas. In contrast, swelling of the legs, body, or face is more prevalent in urban areas (NFHS-3, 2007).

About 34 per cent of the women experienced at least one pregnancy related problem. The proportion was slightly lower among rural women (34 per cent) than among urban women (36 per cent). The major problems reported were 'swelling of hand and feet' (20 per cent), 'paleness' (13 per cent), and 'visual disturbance' (8 per cent). Only 2 per cent reported 'abnormal position of foetus', and 'vaginal bleeding'. About 4 per cent of the women reported 'convulsions' and three per cent reported 'weak or no movement of foetus' (DLHS – 2002-04, 2006).

Place of Delivery

One of the important thrusts of the Reproductive and Child Health Programme is to encourage deliveries in proper hygienic conditions under the supervision of trained health professionals. Deliveries are largely conducted by untrained personnel and in unhygienic conditions; both contribute significantly to poor maternal health.

A 1984-85 study of traditional birth attendants (Sharma and Bali, 1989) in slums in Delhi reveals that, among intranatal practices, as many as 80 per cent did not wash their hands before delivery and two-third used an unsterilized (but fresh) blade to cut the cord. This is quite consistent with a hospital based study of neonates with tetanus which reports that in all cases, unsterilized blades, knives or broken glass were used to cut the cord (Kumar *et al.*, 1988).

The National Population Policy (NPP), adopted by the Government of India in 2000 (Ministry of Health and Family Welfare, 2000), reiterates the Government's commitment to the safe motherhood programme within the wider context of reproductive health. Among the national socio-demographic goals for 2010 specified by the policy, several goals pertain to safe motherhood, 80 per cent of all deliveries should take place in institutions by 2010, hundred per cent deliveries should be attended by trained personnel, and the maternal mortality ratio should be reduced to a level below 100 per 100,000 live births.

Less than 40 per cent of births in India take place in health facilities. The majority of the institutional deliveries were conducted in private institutions (22 per cent of total deliveries) as against in government institution 19 per cent of total deliveries. A large proportion of the births (59 per cent) took place at home More than half take place in the woman's own home and 9 per cent take place in the parents' home. With regard to deliveries at home, the proportion of deliveries in a woman's own home increases and the proportion in her parents' home decreases with age and birth order. Mother's education and household wealth both have a strong negative association with deliveries at home (NFHS-3, 2007).

The percentage of births occurring in health institutions is higher for younger women under the age of 35 years than for women aged 35 years and above. The percentage of institutional deliveries decreases as parity increases. The proportion of births occurring in a health facility is higher for mothers under 20 years of age and age 20-34 years (38-40 per cent) than for mothers age 35-49 (22 per cent).

Only 22 per cent births of scheduled tribe women take place in institutions as compared to 33 per cent of births to scheduled-caste women, 40 per cent to other backward classes and 54 per cent of births to women from the 'other' castes category.

Institutional deliveries are more common among women who had four or more antenatal check-ups (71 per cent) than among those who had fewer antenatal check-ups. Institutional deliveries are least prevalent among births to women who did not receive any antenatal check-up (11 per cent).

Women with a high standard of living were more likely to give birth in health institutions than women with a low standard of living. The per cent of the institutional deliveries increases substantially with women's education and economic status, though the variation in the institutional deliveries by women's education is much conspicuous than that by women's economic status.

Institutional deliveries, particularly in private health facilities, increase sharply with education and the standard of living. About one-fifth births to non-literate women and nearly 80 per cent births to women who had completed at least 10 or more years of schooling took place at health institutions. One factor contributing to these patterns may be a heightened awareness of the benefits of professional medical care during both pregnancy and delivery among urban, educated women and women in households in the highest wealth quintile.

The availability of a health facility establishes a positive relationship with births at health institutions. About 35 per cent of women give birth at a health institution with availability of health facility within a village compared with 25 per cent of women with non-availability of health facilities in the village.

incidence of anaemia, complications during pregnancy and childbirth and birth weight (Dawn and Mitra, 1990; Iyengar, 1975). These findings have prompted a variety of strategies for supplementation the diets of pregnant women. The most ambitious of these is the Integrated Child Development Service (ICDS) programme, in which pregnant and lactating women are provided supplementary nutrition (500 kilo calories and 25 grams of protein) daily. Unfortunately, though this programme has been implemented for over a decade now, there is little information available on changes in reproductive health indicators in areas served by the programme. The little that is available from service statistics suggests that little more than half (51 per cent) of all pregnant and lactating women eligible for this supplementary nutrition actually receive it (Ministry of Welfare, Dept. of Women and Child Development, 1991). In some states, the situation is worse: for example, both ICDS reports and an assessment of the utilization of ICDS services in Rajasthan (Jain and Agarwal, 1986) put this figure at 40 per cent.

The national anemia prophylaxis programme of iron and folic acid distribution, in which pregnant women are provided with 100 iron and folic acid tablets during pregnancy, was initiated as early as the 1950s. However, both service statistics and sample surveys confirm that this programme has not been very successful. From service statistics, were find that no more than an estimated one-third of all pregnant and lactating women (as estimated from population and birth rate figures for 1988089) have received iron and folic acid supplementation. Even more discouraging are the results of the few sample surveys on antenatal care, particularly in the four large northern states. A village level study in Utter Pradesh (Khan *et al.*, 1988) observed that only seven per cent of all pregnant women received iron and folic acid supplementation (Compared to 26 per cent for the state as a whole as estimated from service statistics). A micro-level evaluation by the Indian

Council of Medical Research has shown that the programme has had little effect on the prevalence of anemia among pregnant women (UNICEF, 1991); worse, there was little difference in the prevalence of anemia between those who were supplied the tablets (88.1 per cent) and those who were not (87.6 per cent). Reasons underlying this range from inadequate supplementation to low acceptance, to poor quality of tablets.

Nutritional deficiencies in women are often exacerbated during pregnancy because of the additional nutrient requirements of foetal growth, so a pregnant woman needs six times more iron than a non-pregnant woman.

Iron deficiency anaemia is the most common micro-nutrient deficiency in the world. It is a major threat to safe motherhood and to the health and survival of infants because it contributes to low birth weight, lowered resistance to infection, impaired cognitive development, and decreased work capacity. The provision of iron and folic acid (IFA) tablets to pregnant women to prevent nutritional anaemia forms an integral part of the safe motherhood services offered as part of the Reproductive and Child Health Programme in India.

65 per cent of mothers received IFA supplements for their most recent birth. IFA coverage is well below average for older women, women with fourth or higher order births, women with no education, Muslim women, and women in households in the lowest wealth quintile. IFA coverage is also lower in rural areas (61 per cent) than in urban areas (76 per cent).

Overall, only 23 per cent of women consumed IFA for at least 90 days. This percentage is universally low among all groups of women except women who have completed 12 years of education or more (56 per cent) and women in households in the highest wealth quintile (49 per cent).

Adequate amount of iron folic acid tablets/syrup (100 or more IFA tablets/syrup) were received by only 20 per cent of women, which is much higher in urban areas (30 per cent) than in rural areas (17 per cent). Women with a high standard of living index were more likely to receive an adequate amount of IFA.

Women with higher parity and from scheduled caste and scheduled tribe background were less likely to received adequate amount of IFA.

Full ANC

Women who received at least three antenatal check-ups, and at least one tetanus toxoid injection and supplementary iron in the form of iron folic acid tablets/syrup daily for 100 days during their pregnancy as recommended by the RCH programme alone are considered to have received full antenatal care.

Only 16 per cent of the women in India received full antenatal care. As expected, the coverage of full antenatal care is very low for non-literate women, women with higher parity, Muslim women, women from scheduled tribes and women with a low standard of living.

Full antenatal coverage is also much lower in rural areas (13 per cent) than that in urban areas (26 per cent). Non-literate women received full antenatal care for 8 per cent of their last birth, whereas 20 per cent of literate women (who had completed 9 years of schooling) and 35 per cent of women who had completed ten years or more of schooling had received the full package. Eight per cent of women with a low standard of living received full antenatal care for their last live/still birth, as compared to 20 per cent of women with medium and 33 per cent of women with a high standard of living.

The coverage varies inversely by parity. About 24 per cent of women received the full course of antenatal are with parity-1 compared to only 6 per cent with parity-4 and above. Only 12 per cent of women from scheduled tribes and schedule castes were received antenatal care compared to 16 per cent of women from other backward classes and 21 per cent of 'other' caste category.

Antenatal care utilization in India varies greatly by state. For some indicators the variation ranges from only marginal coverage to almost complete coverage. For example, the percentage of women who had three or more antenatal care visits ranges from only 17 per cent in Bihar to 96 per cent in Tamil Nadu. In general, the southern and western states and some of the northern states perform uniformly well. Bihar, Rajasthan, Uttar Pradesh, and Jharkhand are large states that perform uniformly poorly. The performance of states in the Northeast Region is mixed; notably, however, except for Sikkim and Manipur, the percentage receiving tetanus toxoid injections is below the national average in all of these states.

ANC Visits in India, half of the pregnant women received **at least three antenatal check-ups** and 38 per cent had four or more check-ups. Seventy two per cent of women in urban areas received three antenatal check-ups compared to only 42 per cent of women in rural areas. The availability of a health facility in the village has made a significant difference to have a minimum three visit for antenatal check-ups. About 48 per cent of the women received three or more antenatal check-ups when the health facility was available in the village compared to 37 per cent of women for whom health facilities were not available in the village.

Data on the timing of first antenatal check-ups show that 40 per cent of the women received their first antenatal check-up in the first trimester of pregnancy, and 26 per cent received their first check-up in the second trimester and the remaining 7 per cent of women received their first check-up in the third trimester.

In India, half of the pregnant women received at least three antenatal check-ups and 38 per cent had four or more check-ups. Seventy two per cent of women in urban areas received three antenatal check-ups compared to only 42 per cent of women in rural areas. The availability of a health facility in the village has made a significant difference to have a minimum three visit for antenatal check-ups. About 48 per cent of the women received three or more antenatal check-ups when the health facility was available in the village compared to 37 per cent of women for whom health facilities were not available in the village.

PLACE OF ANC

Thirty three per cent of women received antenatal check-ups at a government health facility; including 10 per cent through the primary health centre and 9 per cent through the sub-centre, and 30 per cent received antenatal check-ups at a private health facility. Other than this, 5 per cent of women reported that they had received antenatal check-ups at an Indian system of medicine, either government or private.

Younger women were more likely to receive antenatal check-ups at government health facilities. Around 33-36 per cent of women age below 30 years received an antenatal check-up at government health facilities than 22-29 per cent of the women age 30 and above. Thirty-one per cent women from rural areas availed government health facilities for antenatal check-ups that were lower than women in urban areas (37 per cent), and also a high proportion of women (46 per cent) from urban areas avail health facilities for antenatal check-ups than women from rural areas, younger women aged 15-19 years, women of scheduled castes and scheduled tribes and women from low standard of living households received antenatal check-ups at sub-centre and primary health centres. A comparatively high proportion of women who had received antenatal check-ups at government health facilities are literate below high school, 68 per cent of rural women received some kind of antenatal check up. The **availability of health facility** in the village has a direct impact on any antenatal check-up, 73 per cent of women staying in villages with health facilities received any antenatal check-up as against 63 per cent of women belonging villages where there were no health facilities. It was observed that 9 per cent of women received antenatal care at the doorstep in those villages where health facility was not available than only 7 per cent of women from those villages with availability of health facilities. About 37 per cent was from urban areas utilized government health facility for antenatal check-ups, whereas it was 31 per cent from urban areas utilized government health facility for antenatal check-ups. Whereas it was slightly higher among women, who could avail themselves availability of health facilities within the villages.

Antenatal coverage in Tamil Nadu, Kerala, Lakshadweep, Pondicherry, Andhra Pradesh, Dadra and Nagar Haveli, Daman and Diu, Goa, Andaman and Nicobar Islands were 95 per cent or more whereas less than 10 per cent of women received antenatal check ups by ANM/Nurse in Kerala, Goa, Lakshadweep, Arunachal Pradesh, Bihar, Tripura, Nagaland, Delhi, Andhra Pradesh, Jammu and Kashmir, Manipur, Assam and Jharkhand.

Reasons for not Seeking Antenatal Check-Ups

Fifty-seven per cent of the women stated that it was not necessary to have an antenatal check-up. It was surprising to see that a higher proportion of urban women (63 per cent) than rural women (58 per cent) felt that it was not necessary to have an antenatal check-up. Fifty nine per cent of women from villages, which had health facilities, stated that an antenatal check-up was not necessary while, it was 55 per cent of women from those villages where a health facility was not available. About 7 per cent of the women felt that it was not customary to go for antenatal check-ups. Other factors contributing to non-use of antenatal care were that it costs too much (13 per cent), it was situated to far, or there was not transportation (4 per cent) and family did not allow (7 per cent) to avail of antenatal care, not time to go (5 per cent), and another 9 per cent reported lack of knowledge of these services. Only one per cent women reported 'poor quality of services' as the main reason. The figures for those who did not avail an antenatal check-up were nearly the same in urban areas and in rural areas. Six per cent of women from villages with a health facility reported that they had no time to go, and the same number of women reported that their family did not allow them to have antenatal check-ups.

REFERENCES

1. Acsadi, George T.F., and Gwendolyn Johnson-Acsadi, 1990. 'Safe motherhood in South Asia socio-cultural and demographic aspects of maternal health,' Background paper, Safe Motherhood South Asia Conference, Lahore.
2. Agarwal, D.K. and K.N. Agarwal, 1987 'Early childhood mortality in Bihar and Uttar Pradesh', Indian Pediatrics 24, No.8 (August): 627-32.
3. Aras, R., N. Pai, and A. Purandare, 1990. 'Perinatal mortality – a retrospective hospital study', Journal of Obstetrics and Gynaecology 40, No.3 (June), 365-69.
4. Bhardwaj, N. *et al.*, 1990. 'Socio-economic factors affecting weight gain in pregnancy', Journal of Obstetrics and Gynaecology 40, No.3 (June): 327-30
5. Bhatia, J.C., 1988. 'A Study of Maternal Mortality in Anantapur District, Andhra Pradesh, India' Bangalore: Indian Institute of Management.

6. Chatterjee, Meera. 1989. 'Socio-economic and socio-cultural influences on women's nutritional status roles' in C. Gopalan and Suminer Kaur (eds.), Women and Nutrition in India, New Delhi: Nutrition Foundation of India.
7. Dawn, C.S. and Bani Kumar Mitra. 1990. 'Effect of food supplementation on maternal weight gain, low birth weight incidence, infant weight gain and breast feed performance', Journal of Obstetrics and Gynaecology 40, No.3 (June): 313-18.
8. District Level Health Survey (DLHS-2, 2002-04), 2006. 'Reproductive and Child Health', International Institute of Population Sciences (Deemed University), Mumbai.
9. Gopalan, C. 1989. 'Women and nutrition in India–general consideration' , in C. Gopalan and Suminder Kaur (eds.), Women and Nutrition in India, New Delhi: Nutrition Foundation of India.
10. Iyengar, L. 1975. 'Influence of the diet on the outcome of pregnancy in Indian women', in Proceedings of the 9th International Congress of Nutrition, Mexico, 1972, Vol. 2, Karger, Nutrition, pp.48-53.
11. Jain, M.L. and Dinesh Agarwal. 1986. 'Utilization of maternal services in an ICDS BLOCK', Journal of Obstetrics and Gynaecology 36, N.5 (October): 842-44.
12. Kanitkar, Tara and R.K. Sinha, 1989. 'Antenatal care services in five States of India'. In S.N. Singh, M.K. Premi, P.S./ Bhatia and Ashish Bose (eds.), Population Transition in India, Vol. 2, pp.201-11, Delhi: B.R. Publishing Corporation.
13. Kapil, U., 1990. "Promotion of safe motherhood in India," Indian Pediatrics, 27: No.3 (March): pp. 232-238.
14. Khan, M.E. and C.V.S. Prasad, 1983. Under-utilization of health services in rural India: A comparative study of Bihar, Gujarat and Kerala, Baroda: Operations Research Group.
15. Khan, M.E., Richard Anker, S.K. Ghosh Dastidar and Sashi Airathi. 1988. 'Inequalities between men and women in nutrition and family welfare services: an in-dept equiry in an Indian Village', Social Action, 38 (October-December).
16. Kumar, Harsh, S. Aneja, V.K. Prasad, S.K. Arora and D.N. Mulick. 1988. 'Tetanus neonatorum: Clinico-epidemiologicla profile', Indian Pediatrics, 25: No.11 (November): 1054-1057.
17. Mathai, Sharmma, T. 1989, 'Women and the Health System' in C. Gopalan and Suminder Kaur (Eds.), Women and Nutrition in

India, New Delhi, Nutrition Foundation of India.

18. Mehta, A. and K. Jayant. 1981. 'Parinatal Mortality Survey in India (1977-79), Part I, Identification of health intervention needs', Journal of Obstetric Gynaecology 32, No.2 (April): 183-215.

19. Mehta, A., M.E. Khan, R.B. Gupta, M.M. Gandotra and O.S. Ojha. 1983. 'Role of Health services delivery on acceptance of family planning', New Delhi: ICMR, Mimeo.

20. Ministry of Welfare, Dept. of Women and Child Development, 1991. '15th year of ICDS, an overview', New Delhi: Government of India.

21. Ministry of Health and Family Welfare (MOH & FW), 1997. 'Statement of National Population Policy', New Delhi: Government of India.

22. Murthy, G.V., Anil Goswami and Saroja Narayanan. 1990. 'Utilization patterns of antenatal services in an urban slum', Journal Obestetrics and Gynaecology 40, No.1 (February): 42-46.

23. National Family Health Survey of India (NFHS-3). 2007. International Institute of Population Sciences (Deemed University), Mumbai.

24. National Family Health Survey of India (NHFS-1), 1992-93. International Institute for Population Sciences (Deemed University), Bombay.

25. National Family Health Survey of India (NHFS-2), 1998-99. International Institute for Population Sciences (Deemed University), Bombay.

26. Ramachandran, Prema., 1989. 'Lactation-nutrition-fertility interaction', in C. Gopalan and Sluminder Kaur (Eds.), Women and Nutrition in India, New Delhi, Nutrition Foundation of India.

27. Ramalinga Swami, V. 1985. 'The State of Life: Report of the National Seminar on reducing incidence of low birth weight babies in India New Delhi: National Institute of Public Cooperation and Child Development.

28. Royston, Eric and Sue Armstrong. 1989. 'Preventing Maternal Deaths', Geneva: World Health Organization.

29. Sadik, Jafis, 1980. 'Family Planning: improving the Health of Women', Draper Fund Report, 9 (October).

30. Sharma, N. and P. Bali. 1989. 'A comparative study of maternal mortality and morbidity in a teaching hospital of Northern India',

Journal of Obstetric and Gynecology, 38, No.2, p.177-181.

31. Singh, Meharban. 1986. 'Hospital based data on perinatal and neonatal mortality in India,' Indian Pediatrics 23, No.8 (August): 579-584.

32. Singh, Surinder, Jagieet Singh, Sushila Mittal, R.K.D. Goel, Tejbir Singh and S.K. Oberoi. 1988. 'A study of antenatal services in rural areas of district of Bathinda of Punjab', Journal of Obsetrics and Gynaecology 38, No.1 (February): 2-26.

33. Singh, Meharban and V.K. Paul. 1988. 'Strategies to reduce perinatal and neonatal mortality', Indian ediatrics 23, No.6, (June): 499-509.

34. Sokhy, J. 1988. 'Magnitude of problems in India', in Ministry of Health and Family Welfare, The Control of Neonatal Tetanus in India, pp. 16-23, New Delhi, Government of India, quoted in Singh and Paul.

35. Srikantia, S.G. 1989a. 'Nutritional deficiency diseases', in C. Gopalan and Suminder Kaur (eds.), Women and Nutrition in India, New Delhi: Nutrition Foundation of India.

36. Starrs, Ann and Diane Measham. 1990, 'Challenge for the Nineties: Safe Motherhood in South Asia', New York and Washington: The World Bank and Family Care International.

37. Tripathi, A.M. D.K. Agarwarl, K.N. Agarwal, R.R. Devi and S. Cherian. 1987. 'Nutritional status of rural pregnant women and foetal outcome', Indian Pediatrics 24, No.9, (September): 703-712.

38. UNICEF, India. 1991, 'Children and Women in India: A Situation Analysis', New Delhi, UNICEF.

39. World Health Organization (WHO), 1994. 'Health, Population and Development', WHO Position Paper for the International Conference on Population and Development, Cairl, WHO/FHE/94.I, Geneva, World Health Organization.

health care in India with reference to health man power, medical care and community health service infrastructure.

HEALTH MAN POWER

Health Man Power of India is best explained in terms of qualified Medical Doctors registered with the Indian Medical Council, Nurse Mid Wife, Health Assistants, Multi-Purposes Health Workers etc.

At the start of the First Five Year Plan period during the year 1951 there were only 61800 qualified registered allopathic medical practitioners in India. In other words there were only 17.11 doctors per one lakh population. From this poor doctor-population ratio in the year 1951 India could raise the Doctor-population ratio to impressive levels. By the year 2001 there were 56.15 doctors per one lakh population, totaling a large number of 605800 registered allopathic medical practitioners.

Similarly, the Nurse and population ratio too was very poor at the time India attained republichood. It was only 4 nurses per one lakh population. From this poor it raised by the year 2001, to 78 Nurses per lakh population; in other words now per every 126 persons there is one nurse where as previously it was one for every 20,000 persons. (See Table 3.1).

The data on Health Man Power to serve rural areas in India. (Table 3.2) reveals that with the exception of doctors, the required Health Man Power is not adequately commissioned. In other worlds what it means is that the supportive health man power is not available and thus access to equitable health care is denied in rural areas. To reach India's remote villages and thus serve the rural masses these Para-medical staff is essential to extend the primary health care to realize the goal of Health for All.

Table 3.1: Ratio of Allopathic Medical Practitioners & Nurses per 1,00,000 Population in India.

Year	Population in Millions	Ratio per 1,00,000 population	
		Medical Practitioners	Nurses
1951	36.11	17	5
1961	43.92	19	9
1971	54.92	28	14
1981	68.33	39	21
1991	84.33	47	40
2001	99.69	56	78

Source: Central Bureau of Health Intelligence, Directorate of General of Health Services, Ministry of Health and Family Welfare Nirman Bhavan, New Delhi – 110011.

Table 3.2: India's Health Man Power

	Position Required	In Position	Man Power Surplus/ shortage	Popula-tion Served
Doctors	22842	25724	+2882	28831
Block Extension Education	6743	1035	-5708	716579
Health Assistants (M)	22842	19927	2915	37219
Health Assistants (F)	22842	19855	2989	37354
Health Workers/MPW (M)	137311	71053	66258	10438
Health Workers/MPW (F)	160153	137407	22746	5398
Nurse-mid-wife	44143	27336	16807	37131

Source: Central Bureau of Health Intelligence, Directorate of General of Health Services, Ministry of Health and Family Welfare Nirman Bhavan, New Delhi – 110011.

Medical care intervention and its equity can not be achieved by mere establishment of hospitals, community health centres and primary health centres. It can be achieved only when adequate health man power is provided.

However, there is some misconception in this policy. Some States believed that by providing professionally qualified medical doctors in adequate numbers would enable the people to get the required medical attention and thus health care equity can be achieved. Whereas, a few other States stressed the need for para-medics who would serve as first contact grass-root medical interventionists to provide the primary health care inputs and thus the primary requirement of the rural masses and health care equity can be achieved.

The experience of the states which have achieved better health status shows that the strategy of emphasis on primary health needs through the para-medical grass-root health workers has resulted in improved health status. These states have taken care in providing adequate (if not required number of) number of qualified doctors and equally importance and stress was laid on such gross-root para-medics as Nurse-Midwife and Multipurpose Health Workers and also on the importance on health educators. Table 3.3 presents the details of health manpower statistics of the different States under reference.

Our examination shows that Kerala which registered better Health status in India has laid importance not only on doctors but also on Nurse-mid Wife and Multipurpose Health Workers. On the contrary the Orissa State which has poor health status record in terms of larger infant mortality rate (which reflects poor mother and child care) emphasized on qualified medical doctors alone and neglected the nurse-mid wives and the need for health assistants. States like West Bengal have laid emphasis on both professional doctors and as well as para-medics. States such as Rajasthan which was lagging in health status in terms of IMR have realized the need for grass-root para-medics, particularly the Nurse-midwife and female MPHW along with professional medical doctors and heath educators

Table 3.3: Health Man Power in Rural Area (2003).

States	Doctors		BEE		Health Ass. Male		Health Ass. Female LHV		HW/MPW (M)		MPW/ ANM (F)		Nurses Midwife	
	Required	Position	Required	Position	Required	Position	Required	Position	Required	Position	Required	Position	Required	Position
Andhra Pradesh	1386	1495	454	37	1386	1285	1386	1553	10568	6756	11954	10888	2919	1039
Karnataka	1676	1901	736	440	1676	1122	1676	1161	8143	4048	9819	8270	3419	2955
Kerala	944	1239	160	151	944	847	944	858	5094	3394	6038	5396	1679	1907
Maharastra	1768	3160	348	305	1768	2294	1768	1536	9725	7877	11493	11432	4225	2538
Orissa	1352	2351	329	284	1352	168	1352	998	5297	337	7279	6944	2451	386
Rajasthan	1674	1537	232	127	1674	714	1674	1318	9926	3374	11600	11791	3515	9212
Tamil Nadu	1436	2648	382	350	1436	3005	1436	1679	8682	3765	10118	10538	1940	167
West Bengal	1262	1841	768	680	1262	1689	1262	1447	8126	8652	9388	8126	1955	3134
India	**22842**	**25724**	**6743**	**1035**	**22842**	**19927**	**22842**	**19855**	**137311**	**71053**	**160153**	**137407**	**44143**	**27366**

Source: Central Bureau of Health Intelligence, Directorate of General of Health Services, Ministry of Health and Family Welfare, Nirman Bhavan, New Delhi-110011.

and made provisions for the same by the year 2001. The State of Andhra Pradesh however, has neglected the sector of rural Health man-power particularly with regard to the para-medics who would bridge the gap of health care equity and thus the state has paid dearly in terms of poor health status and high infant mortality rates.

The significance of the reach of the para-medics on attaining health care quality can be understood by examining the Table 3.4. Table 3.4 presents the details of rural population and health man-power ratio. This ratio explains the population served by the each of the health workers/ professional. In other words it explains the access and equity of health care to the rural masses.

For instance, the State like Orissa which has high infant mortality rate has a better doctor-population ratio (1:13,275 persons) where as it has a poor nurse-midwife and population ratio (1:80,856 persons). A State like Orissa needs more no. of nurse-midwives to promote better mother & child care in rural areas than doctors. A nurse-midwife is more accessible and acceptable to poor rural masses than the services of doctors which is expensive. The state of Rajasthan though laid emphasis on nurse-midwife and female multipurpose health workers has neglected the need for professional doctors, health educators and health assistants. The State of Andhra Pradesh stressed only on multipurpose heath workers and neglected the professionals like doctors and para-medics such as nurse-midwives. The doctor-population ratio is 36.939 persons which is eight thousand persons higher than the national average. Similarly, its nurse-midwife ratio is 53,151 persons and the national average ratios are only 27,131 persons. Naturally, such misplaced priorities and strategies have pushed the heath status of the people of Andhra Pradesh to the level of concern and dismay. In the State of Kerala the doctor population ratio is 19,025 persons; female multipurpose health workers ratio is 4368 persons and the nurse-midwife ratio is 12,361 persons.

When these ratios are compared with National level ratios States like Andhra Pradesh and West Bengal have poor doctor-population ratios; States like Tamil Nadu, Andhra Pradesh, and Orissa have poor nurses-midwife – population ratios. States like Andhra Pradesh, Maharastra, Rajasthan and Kerala have not paid attention to the importance of health educators. These states with the exception of Kerala have rather poor female literacy level. Kerala State, which has very high female literacy level, understandably overlooked the need for health educators as it has a high literacy level. States like Karnataka, Tamil Nadu and West Bengal have paid due attention to the role and importance of health educators. These details are presented in Table 3.4.

MEDICAL CARE

The provisions of Medical Care are generally explained with reference to number of Hospitals and hospitals beds available and their ratio.

At the beginning of the First Five Year Plan period there were only seven allopathic hospitals per million population and this situation continued upto Fourth Five Year Plan. Since then there is considerable improvement in Hospital population ratio. Now this ratio is 15 allopathic hospitals per one million populations. Table 3.5 presents the details of the growth in the number of allopathic hospitals since 1952 to 2002 and as well as beds & population ratio.

Table 3.6 reveals the distribution of allopathic hospitals, dispensaries and hospital beds by rural and urban area wise. The data shows that there is greater urban bias in the location of allopathic hospitals, as a prepondering majority of them (80.77 per cent) are located in urban

Table 3.4: Rural Population & Health Man Power Ratio (2003).

States	Rural Population 2001	Doctors	BEE	Health Ass. Male	Health Ass. LHV Female	MPW Male	MPW/ ANM Female	Nurse Midwife
Andhra Pradesh	5,52,23,944	36,939	14,92,539	42,976	35,560	8,174	5,072	53,151
Karnataka	34814100	18314	79123	31029	29986	8600	4210	11781
Kerala	23571484	19025	156103	27829	27473	6945	4368	12361
Maharastra	55732513	17637	182730	24295	36284	9289	5281	21959
Orissa	31210602	13275	109896	185777	31273	92613	4495	80856
Rajasthan	43267678	28151	340690	60599	32828	12824	3670	4697
Tamil Nadu	34869286	13168	99627	11604	20768	9261	3309	208798
West Bengal	57734690	37320	84904	34183	39900	6742	7105	18422
India	**741660293**	**28831**	**129933**	**37219**	**37354**	**10738**	**5398**	**27131**

Source: Central Bureau of Health Intelligence, Directorate of General of Health Services, Ministry of Health and Family Welfare, Nirman Bhavan, New Delhi-110011.

areas and naturally same is the situation with regard to hospital beds. However, in the case of the dispensaries there is slight rural bias.

Table 3.5: India's Medical Care in India.

Year	No. of Allopathic Hospitals	No. of Hospitals per Million Population	All type of Beds per lakh Population
1952	2,694	7	32
1962	3,054	7	57
1972	3,862	7	54
1982	6,804	10	83
1992	11,174	13	95
2002	15,393	15	89

Source: Central Bureau of Health Intelligence, Directorate of General of Health Services, Ministry of Health and Family Welfare, Nirman Bhavan, New Delhi-110011.

Table 3.6: Allopathic Hospitals by Area (2003)

	Rural	%	Urban	%	Total
Hospitals	3450	19.23	10284	80.77	12734
Hospitals Beds	59061	10.64	496268	89.36	555329
Dispensaries	11045	51.80	10278	48.2	21323
Dispensaries Beds	15671	53.41	13670	46.32	29341

Source: Central Bureau of Health Intelligence, Directorate of General of Health Services, Ministry of Health and Family Welfare, Nirman Bhavan, New Delhi-110011.

An examination of Hospital based medical intervention levels reveals interesting trends. Our analysis (Table 3.7) indicates that with the exception of Kerala in all other states under reference there were fewer hospital based medical intervention in relation to population they serve and it is particularly true with regard to rural population; and particularly in the case of States like Orissa, Rajasthan, which recorded lower health status.

In Kerala hospital based medical intervention was available for every 15169 population and hospital bed-population ratio was 325 persons. In other words for every 325 people one hospital bed was available. On the contrary in Orissa and Rajasthan the situation was dismaying. In these states Hospital-Population ratios were 1,34,458 and 4,90,593 respectively. Similarly Hospitals bed-population ratios were 3064 and 3175 persons respectively. Interestingly, States like West Bengal and Tamil Nadu, Karnataka which have shown better health status also have fewer hospital based interventions. Their hospital and population ratios were 1,96,973; 135743 and 1,73,235 person respectively; and the hospital bed population ratios were 1464, 1135 and 1719 person respectively.

The case of Maharastra, which has better health status than the above states is however different. It has relatively better hospital and population ratios. But it was highly urban biased. The hospital and population ratio in Maharastra was 26,441 persons and the hospital bed and population ratio was found to be 920 persons. There were only 353 hospitals in rural areas as against 3093 hospitals in the urban areas.

The urban bias in hospital based Medical intervention was not limited to Maharastra alone. It was found in other states too. For instance, in Karnataka the rural-urban ratio of hospitals was ten. In other words for every ten hospitals in urban areas there was one hospital in rural areas. Similarly, in Rajasthan the ratio was seven; in Tamil Nadu it was four and in West Bengal it was three; and in Andhra Pradesh it was two; in the case of Kerala there was no rural-urban distinction.

Table 3.7: Number of Allopathic Hospitals & Beds by Area & Ratio to Population (2003).

States	Hospitals			Ratio	Beds			Ratio
	Rural	Urban	Total		Rural	Urban	Total	
Andhra Pradesh	1060	2073	3133	23,547	14187	55591	69778	1,057
Karnataka	25	268	293	173235	3015	35464	38479	1319
Kerala	—	—	2099	15169	—	—	97949	325
Maharastra	353	3093	3446	26441	5961	93101	99062	920
Orissa	100	173	273	134458	1498	10482	11980	3064
Rajasthan	13	100	113	490593	1150	16309	17459	3175
Tamil Nadu	89	319	408	135743	4235	44545	48780	1135
West Bengal	105	306	411	196793	4809	50470	55279	1464
India	**2450**	**1028**	**15393**	**66758**	**59061**	**496268**	**683545**	**1503**

Source: Central Bureau of Health Intelligence, Directorate of General of Health Services, Ministry of Health and Family Welfare, Nirman Bhavan, New Delhi-110011.

To minimize the urban bias in hospital based medical intervention, dispensaries with beds were provided to reach the needy (Table 3.8). In this regard Maharastra was exemplary. There were 2495 dispensaries with 2615 beds. This example was followed by Orissa and Karnataka States and to a smaller extent by Tamil Nadu and Andhra Pradesh. These dispensaries were in addition to primary health centres. The details are presented in Table 3.8.

Table 3.8: Number of Allopathic Dispensaries & Beds by Area (2003).

States	Dispensaries			Beds		
	Rural	Urban	Total	Rural	Urban	Total
Andhra Pradesh	109	25	134	—	—	—
Karnataka	563	234	797	809	354	1163
Kerala	41	13	54	108	68	176
Maharastra	2495	3357	5852	2615	3193	5808
Orissa	1196	63	1259	146	136	282
Rajasthan	—	268	268	—	134	134
Tamil Nadu	147	365	512	138	140	278
West Bengal	132	74	206	—	—	—
India	**11045**	**10278**	**22291**	**15671**	**13670**	**29662**

Source: Central Bureau of Health Intelligence, Directorate of General of Health Services, Ministry of Health and Family Welfare, Nirman Bhavan, New Delhi-110011.

In terms of providing access to hospital based medical intervention by Bed care (of all types such as Hospitals, Dispensaries, and Sanatorium) Kerala stands first and the State of Orissa stands last. In the case of Kerala bed and population ratio was 290 persons and with regard to Orissa it was found to be 2,188 persons. It may be pointed out here that, though the health status was better in the case of West Bengal, Tamil Nadu the parity in their population

& Bed ratios was also higher. In West Bengal the ratio was one bed for every 1143 persons; and in Tamil Nadu it was 908 persons. These details are shown in Table 3.9.

Table 3.9: Number of Beds All Types & Population Ratio (2003).

States	No. of Beds All Type	Pop. Served Ratio
Andhra Pradesh	75910	972
Karnataka	56558	897
Kerala	109759	290
Maharastra	128076	711
Orissa	16780	2188
Rajasthan	44373	1249
Tamil Nadu	61000	908
West Bengal	70820	1143
India	**91820**	**1124**

All Type = Hospitals, Dispensaries, PHCs, Santorum.

Source: Central Bureau of Health Intelligence, Directorate of General of Health Services, Ministry of Health and Family Welfare, Nirman Bhavan, New Delhi – 110011.

COMMUNITY HEALTH SERVICES

The problem of inequity and urban bias in the progress of medical care is addressed by the concept of Primary Health Care. It may be pointed out here that Bhore Committee (1948), stressed the need for primary health care and this was reiterated by several committees in the later years.

Though the need for primary health was conceived very early in the annals of modern India not much of attention was paid in this direction to provide primary rural health/ medical care. In fact until the Fifth Five Year Plan period the provision of medical care to rural areas has not gained momentum. It was the call of Alma Ata Declaration in 1978 which has stimulated the Government of India to pay greater attention to primary health care. The provision of minimum needs progress of this plan period has strengthened the provision of primary health care in India.

India is a signatory to the Alma Ata Declaration of 1978 and had committed to attaining "Health for All" by 2000AD through the Primary Health Care approach. The establishment of Primary Health Centres in India started as early as in 1952, and over the last five decades it has undergone several changes to meet the increasing demand for health care services. Until the Eighth Five Year Plan, the emphasis was on the expansion of the health care establishment. However, during the Eighth and subsequent plans the emphasis was mainly on consolidation of existing health infrastructure rather than on expansion. "The trust has been on qualitative improvement in the health services through strengthening of physical facilities like provision of essential equipment, supply of essential drugs and consumables, construction of buildings and staff quarters, filling up of vacant posts of medical and para-medical staff and in-service training of staff."

The National Health Policy stressed on the provision of preventive, promotive and rehabilitative health services to the people thereby making a shift from medical care to health care. The delivery of Primary Health Care is the foundation of the rural health care system and is an integral part of the national health care system. In the rural areas, services are provided through a network of integrated health and family welfare system and the health programmes have been restructured and reoriented from time to time to meet the objectives of the National Health Policy.

The health care delivery system in India can be grouped into four types: (a) public sector, including Government runs hospitals, dispensaries and health centres, (b) those run by non-governmental organizations (NGO), (c) organized private sector, and (d) informal private sector comprising faith healers and herbalists etc. Studies have shown that the Government is by far the dominant source of health care such as immunizations, antenatal care, family planning services, and infectious disease control In line with this, the Ministry of Health and Family Welfare (MoHFW), Government of India (GoI) is implementing a Reproductive and Child Health (RCH) programme in the country. Under this programme, a range of reproductive and child health services is being provided through a network of Government health care establishments. The programme also aims to strengthen health infrastructure in terms of trained staff, equipment and supplies to enhance the facilities to provide good quality RCH services.

The number of different facilities provided varies from district to district due to the differences in the population in each district as well as due to the differences in adherence to population norms. The population norms for some of the facilities are given below:

Centre	Population Norm	
	Plain Area	Hilly/Tribal Area
Sub-centre	5,000	3,000
PHC	30,000	20,000
CHC	120,000	80,000

Sub-centres are peripheral contact points between the Primary Health Care System and the community. One male Multipurpose Worker and one female Multipurpose Worker/ANM are expected to be appointed at each facility.

A PHC, on the other hand, is the first contact point between the village community and the Medical Officer. A PHC is expected to have a Medical Office and 14 para-medical and other staff. It acts as a referral unit for 5-6 Sub-centres. It should have 4-6 beds for patients. The activities of the PHCs involve curative, preventive, promotive and family welfare services.

CHCs are basically referral centres for PHCs approximately at the rate of 1:4. Its man-power strength includes four medical specialists (Surgeon, Physician, Gynaecologist and Paediatrician) supported by 21 para-medical and other staff. It also should have 30 indoor beds with one OT, X-ray, labour room and laboratory facilities.

As a consequence of these policy recommendations India launched community health centres and primary health centres and sub-centres to cater the health/medical needs of the rural masses.

Community health centres serve as secondary referral centres; and primary health centres serve as first referral centres. Each of the community health centres serves an approximate population of one lakh people. The primary health centre will cater to the needs of twenty to thirty thousand population. A sub-centres will serve a population of five thousand population. Each of the community health centres covers four primary health centres and similarly each of the primary health centres covers six sub-centres. The growth and distribution of these community health services are presented in the Table 3.10.

To provide better and equitable health care and medical interventions in rural areas more systematic and determined efforts were made from Sixth Five Year Plan period onwards. These efforts, were the result of recommendations of various committees and Alma Ata Declaration. As a result every state has provided for Primary Health Centre, Sub centres and Community Health Centres and have made a steady progress. But the progress and emphasis in providing these services have varied from State to State. These details are presented in Tables 3.11, 3.12 & 3.13.

Table 3.10: Community Health Services.

Plan Period	CHC	PHC	Sub-centres
I Five Year Plan	—	725	—
II Five Year Plan	—	2565	—
III Five Year Plan	—	4631	
IV Five Year Plan	—	5283	33509
V Five Year Plan	214	5484	47112
VI Five Year Plan	761	9115	84376
VII Five Year Plan	1910	18671	130165
VIII Five Year Plan	2633	22149	136258
As on 31.3.2001	3043	22842	137311

Source: Central Bureau of Health Intelligence, Directorate of General of Health Services, Ministry of Health and Family Welfare, Nirman Bhavan, New Delhi-110011.

The States of Karnataka and Rajasthan, which were lagging in rural based Medical intervention, have shown greater vigour in providing Primary Health Centres to serve the rural areas. They have large number of Primary Health Centres today. For instance, there were 1676 Primary Health Centres in Karnataka as on 2001 year and in Rajasthan there were 1674 Primary Health Centres by the year 2001. In rest of the states Primary Health Centres were provided with greater zeal during the Seventh Five Year Plan period; where as States like Maharastra and West Bengal were consistent right from Sixth Five Year Plan period onwards. Unlike the other states under reference these States (viz. West Bengal and Maharashtra) have provided larger number of Primary Health Centres during the Sixth Five Year Plan period itself. (See Table 3.11)

Table 3.11: Primary Health Centres - Progress.

States	VIth Plan 1981-85	VIIth Plan 1985-90	VIIIth Plan 1992-97	IXth Plan 1997-01 (No. function by 2001)
Andhra Pradesh	555	1263	1335	1386
Karnataka	365	1142	1601	1676
Kerala	199	908	938	944
Maharastra	1539	1671	1695	1768
Orissa	484	875	1102	1352
Rajasthan	448	1048	1516	1674
Tamil Nadu	436	1386	1436	1436
West Bengal	1172	1250	1262	1262
India	**9115**	**18671**	**22149**	**22842**

Source: Central Bureau of Health Intelligence, Directorate of General of Health Services, Ministry of Health and Family Welfare, Nirman Bhavan, New Delhi-110011.

A more recent all India survey on rural health facilities presents a revealing picture. The survey was based on the key features of 9688 PHCs and their functioning.

Out of the total Primary Health Centres, 89 per cent are functioning from their own building. In about 12 per cent of the Primary Health Centres there is regular maintenance. In 62-66 per cent of the PHCs, there is electricity and water facility (at least well water). A little more than two-thirds of the Primary Health Centres have at lest one bed and there is provision for admitting in-patients. At least 46 per cent of the Primary Health Centres have a labour room and a test laboratory each. The communication and transportation facilities are available with only a small proportion of Primary Health Centres, as only 20 per cent and 23 per cent reported having a telephone and functional vehicle respectively. In half of the

Primary Health Centres there are staff quarters for the Medical Officer.

Table 3.12: Progress of Sub-Centres

States	VIth Plan 1981-85	VIIth Plan 1985-90	VIIIth Plan 1992-97	IXth Plan 1997-01
Andhra Pradesh	6129	7894	10568	10568
Karnataka	4964	7793	8143	8143
Kerala	2270	5094	5044	5094
Maharastra	6391	9248	9725	9725
Orissa	4127	5927	5927	5927
Rajasthan	3790	8000	9400	9926
Tamil Nadu	5860	8681	8681	8682
West Bengal	6100	7873	7573	8126
India	**84376**	**130165**	**136258**	**137311**

Source: Central Bureau of Health Intelligence, Directorate of General of Health Services, Ministry of Health and Family Welfare, Nirman Bhavan, New Delhi-110011.

There is not a single category of staff that is available in all the surveyed Primary Health Centres. Seventy-eight per cent of the Primary Health Centres have at least one Medical Officer, implying that almost two in ten Primary Health Centres function without a Medical Officer. In less than one-sixth of the Primary Health Centres, there is a lady Medical Officer on the staff. In 85 per cent of the Primary Health Centres, at least one female health worker is available. Sixty-five per cent of the Primary Health Centres have a Laboratory Technician. Primary Health Centres not only lack staff, but they also lack in trained staff. All the Primary Health Centres do not have at least one medical or paramedical staff trained in various components of the RCH Programme. As low as 15 per cent of the PHCs have Medical Officers trained in sterilization and MTP respectively and 47 per cent trained in RCH integrated training. The training status of paramedical staff is not satisfactory, as 43 per cent to 69 per cent of the Primary Health Centres have at least one paramedical person trained in IUD insertion, Control of Diarrhoeal Diseases/Oral Rehydration Therapy, Universal Immunization Programme, Child Survival and Safe Motherhood and Reproductive and Child Health.

Under the Reproductive and Child Health progamme, Primary Health Centres are provided few kits of instruments/ drugs. About half of the Primary Health Centres had not received IUD insertion kit and Normal Delivery kit. The Essential Obstetric Care drug kit was received by only one-third of the surveyed Primary Health Centres. The Nirodh, oral pills and measles vaccines were received by 48 per cent to 59 per cent and IFA (large) tablets were received by 57 per cent of the Primary Health Centres. Seventy-one per cent of PHCs had stock of ORS packets on the day of survey. Data on the availability of different equipment shows that 64-76 per cent of the Primary Health Centres have adult and infant weighing machines. The three sets of equipment necessary for storing and carrying the vaccines, deep freezer, vaccine carrier and refrigerator are available in 53, 68 and 16 per cent of Primary Health Centres respectively. The autoclave and steam sterilizer drum necessary for sterilization of the needles and syringes are available in at least 70 per cent of the Primary Health Centres.

Though Primary Health Centres are expected to provide safe abortion services, the MTP suction is available in less than one-third of the Primary Health Centres. However, the BP instrument is available at 88 per cent of the PHCs.

Though all the Primary Health Centres are expected to provide facilities for each component of RCH such as, institutional delivery, safe abortion, neonatal care, and contraceptive services, only a small proportion of Primary

Health Centres provide these services. Only 58 per cent of the surveyed PHCs in India conducted deliveries, 6 per cent PHCs conducted MTP and 22 per cent PHCs provided neonatal care.

Around 65 per cent and 41 per cent of PHCs in India conducted IUD insertion and sterilization respectively. The component of critical inputs when studied separately shows that 41 per cent of the Primary Health Centres have adequate equipment.

However, the situation of infrastructure, supply and staff is also not encouraging, for example; only 32-48 per cent of the Primary Health Centres are adequately equipped with these. Inadequacy reigns high in the training of medical and para-medical staff where only 20 per cent of the PHCs are adequately staffed with trained personnel.

Table 3.13: Progress of Community Health Centres.

States	VIth Plan 1981-85	VIIth Plan 1985-90	VIIIth Plan 1992-97	IXth Plan 1997-01
Andhra Pradesh	27	46	207	219
Karnataka	98	156	242	249
Kerala	4	54	80	105
Maharastra	147	290	300	351
Orissa	59	92	157	157
Rajasthan	76	185	261	263
Tamil Nadu	30	72	72	72
West Bengal	23	87	89	99
India	**761**	**1910**	**2633**	**3043**

Source: Central Bureau of Health Intelligence, Directorate of General of Health Services, Ministry of Health and Family Welfare, Nirman Bhavan, New Delhi-110011.

The provision of rural based second referral level medical intervention through Community Health Centres gained momentum during the Seventh and particularly during Eight

Five Year Plan periods. Here too some States had their own priorities and strategies of Health care intervention. The details are presented in Table 3.13.

States like Tami Nadu, West Bengal, and Kerala have given lesser priority to Community Health Centres and they have provided fewer centres. For instance, Tamil Nadu has not provided for Community Health Centres after Seventh Five Year Plan period; similarly West Bengal too has given minimum priority. On the other hand, the other States under reference, have been giving greater emphasis on Community Health Centres to provide equitable health care from Seventh Plan period onwards. States like Orissa, Rajasthan, and Karnataka were particularly laid emphasis on the provision of Community Health Centres. (See Table 3.13).

REFERECES

1. Government of India, *Bulletin on Rural Health Statistics in India*, June 1998, Rural Health Division, Directorate General of Health Services, Ministry of Health and Family Welfare, Government of India, New Delhi, 1998.
2. Bhat, Ramesh, 1995, *Private Health Care in India*: The *private/ public mix in health care in India*, IHPP reprint series. International Health Policy Program, Washington, D. C. World Bank. 3. World Bank, *Improving Women's Health in India*, Washington D. C. 1996.
3. Central Bureau of Health Intelligence. 2003. 'Health Information of India', Directorate of General of Health Services, Ministry of Health and Family Welfare, Nirman Bhavan, New Delhi-110011.

CHAPTER 4

The Setting and Socio-economic Profile of Stakeholders

In the present chapter an attempt is made to analyze the access to communication, education and health services and facilities to the select communities and to portray their socio-economic characteristics. For this purpose this Chapter is divided into four Sections.

At the outset the portrayal of the universe, namely, Anantapur District is presented. The portrayal depicts background characteristics, details of population, communication, education, health services and facilities and the reproductive practices.

In the Second Section the details of the population, communication, education, health services and facilities present in the study revenue mandals; and the details of the study villages are presented.

The Third Section portrays the socio-economic characteristics of the respondents under study.

The analysis pertaining to respondents' access to communication, education and health services and facilities is presented in the Fourth Section.

SECTION - I

The universe of the study, Anantapur District is located in the State of Andhra Pradesh. Andhra Pradesh is divided into three distinct socio-cultural regions namely, Coastal Andhra, Telangana and Rayalaseema regions. Rayalaseema region is backward and chronically drought prone region. Anantapur District is located in this region.

SALIENT FEATURES OF THE ANANTAPUR DISTRICT

Historical Background

Anantapur District was formed in the year 1882 having been separated from Bellary District. Later on, it was expanded with the addition of Revenue Mandals of Kadiri, Mudigubba, Nallamada, N.P. Kunta, Talupula, Nallacheruvu, O.D.Cheruvu, Tanakal, Amadagur and Gandlapenta (previous Kadiri Taluk) from Cuddapah District in the year 1910. During the year 1956, the present Revenue Mandals of Rayadurg, D.Hirehal, Kanekal, Bommanahal and Gummagatta of Bellary District were added to Anantapur District.

Boundaries and Topography

Anantapur District lies between 13'-40' and 15'-15' Northern Latitude and 76'-50' and 78'-30' Eastern Longitude. It is bounded by Bellary, Kurnool District on the North, Cuddapah and Kolar District (of Karnataka) on South East and North respectively. The District is roughly oblong in shape, the longer side running north to south with a portion of Chitradurg District of Karnataka State intruding into it from west between Kundurpi and Amarapuram Mandals. The District may be divided into **three** Natural Divisions. They are: 1) Northern Mandal of Rayadurg, Kanekal, Beluguppa Gooty, Guntakal, Vajrakarur,

Uravakonda, Vidapanakal, Yadiki, Tadipatri, Putlur and Yellanur containing larger areas of Black Cotton soils (2) Kalyandurg, Kambadur, Settur, Brahmasamudram, Ramagiri, Kanaganapalli, C.K.Palli, Dharmavaram, Bathalapalli, Tadimarri, Mudigubba, Anantapur, Kudair, Pamidi and Peddavadugur in the center which are mainly made up of arid Treeless, expanse of poor Red Soils, (3) High Level Land of Penukonda, Roddam, Somandepalli, Hindupur, Lepakshi, Chilamathur, Madakasira, Rolla, Gudibanda and Agali which connects with Mysore plateau at higher elevation of the rest of the District. This part has average sandy red soils of normal productivity.

Forests

The District is not rich in the Forest Wealth. The name 'Forest' in Anantapur District does not indicate any dense tree population with thick foliage The Forests in the District is thin and scanty. The Muchukota Hills about 35 KMs. in length run from North of Gooty Town upto extreme Southern Corner of Tadipatri and Yadiki Mandals. Another line of Hills starts from West of Gooty Mandal and run 80 kilometers called by name Nagasamudram Hills. The Mallappakonda Range begins at Dharmavaram and runs into Karnataka State.

The Penukonda Range which starts in the South of Dharmavaram through Penukonda and Hindupur proceeds to Karnataka State. In Madakasira, the hills divide Rolla and Agali Mandals into Southern and Northern portions. There are numerous isolated Peaks and Rocky Clusters which are devoid of any vegetation. The heights of some of these Hill Ranges are given below:

Mallappakonda four Miles to	
North of Bukkapatnam	- 3002 feet
Penukonda	- 3091 feet

Kundurpi Durgam - 2996 feet

Madakasira - 2936 feet

Mineral Resources

Barites, High Grade Lime Stones, Iron ore and steatite are the minerals occurring in the District. There are however, no large sized minerals occurring in the District. Gold is found to occur in the District. Diamonds are also known to be available.

There are two Cement Factories in Tadipatri Mandal one in the Public Sector and the other in Private Sector. The construction work of L & T Factory is completed and started production.

Rivers

The important river in the District is Pennar. Jayamangala, Chitravathi, Vedavathi or Hagari are the other significant rivers in the District.

Apart from these, streams like Kushavathi in Chilamathur Mandal Swarnamukhi in Agali Mandal Maddileru in Nallamada, Kadiri and Mudigubba Mandals Pandameru in Kanaganipalli, Raptadu, Anantapur B.K.Samudram and Singanamala Mandals Papagni in Tanakal Mandal are important water supply sources to various large and medium irrigation tanks in the District.

There is one Major Irrigation Project T.B.P.H.L.C., and three Medium Irrigation Projects. 1. Upper Pennar Project, 2. Bhairavanithippa Project, 3. Chennarayaswamy Gudi.

Rainfall and Climate

The District has a dubious distinction of receiving the second lowest rainfall in the country! The normal rainfall of the district is 552.0 MMs., by which it secures least rainfall when compared to Rayalaseema and other parts of Andhra Pradesh.

The Geographical position of the Peninsula render it, the driest part of the State and hence, Agriculture conditions are more often precarious, the District is deprived of both the monsoons and subjected to droughts due to bad seasons and thus is chronically drought prone.

The District of Anantapur has a fairly good elevation which provides the District with tolerable climate throughout the year. There is a gradual rise in Hindupur, Parigi, Lepakshi, Chilamathur, Agali, Rolla and Madakasira Mandals in the South to join the Karnataka Plateau where the average elevation is about 2000 feet is above the mean sea level. It is about 1100 feet at Anantapur and the lowest 900 feet is at Tadipatri.

Soils and Land Utilization

The soils in Anantapur District are predominantly red. Thus 76 per cent are red soils, 24 per cent are black soils. The total geographical area of the District is 19.13 lakh Hects. (Table 4.1.1)

The cultivated area of the District is 10.44 Lakh Hect. Out of which 9.00 Lakh hectares are under Kharif and 1.44 Lakh hectares, is under Rabi Season during the year 2002-2003.

The District occupies the lowest position in respect of Irrigation facilities with only 14.98% of the gross cropped area during 2002-2003 out of the gross irrigated area of 1.56 Lakh Hects. During 2002-2003 canals accounted for 13.23 per cent tanks, 1.39 per cent (tube wells) 64.83 per cent wells 19.22 per cent and other sources 1.33 per cent.

Table 4.1.1: Anantapur District Area Profile.

Sl. No.	Item	Unit	
1.	Geographical Area	Sq.Km.	19130
2.	Forest Coverage	%	10.30
3.	Normal Rainfall	M.M.	553
4.	Gross Cropped Area	Lakh in Hectors	10.44
5.	Gross Irrigated Area	Lakh in Hectors	1.56
6.	Gross Irrigated Percentage to Total	(%)	14.94

Source: 1. Hand Book of Anantapur District Statistics, Anantapur, 2002-03.
2. Census of India, 2001.

Revenue Administrative Divisions

The District is divided into 3 Revenue Divisions consisting of 63 Revenue Mandals (Anantapur Division, 20; Dharmavaram Division, 17; and Penukonda Division, 26).

There are 940 inhabited villages, out of a total 964 Revenue Villages of the District. The number of villages in population size group of 500 to 1999 forms 36.06 per cent of the total inhabited villages. The size group of 2000 to 4999 forms 38.19 per cent and the size group of 5000 to 9999 forms 12.34 per cent only out of total villages, while 85 villages (9.04 per cent) of total inhabited villages are having population less than 500. There are 26 villages with more than 10000 population excluding Towns. There are 10 Towns in Anantapur District as per 2001 Census. The unique feature however is that most of the revenue villages have constituent villages. Thus a revenue village often consists of a Constellation of hamlet villages. The hamlet villages thus are not the units for administrative sanctions, grants or for statistical records. Thus the District of Anantapur comprises 940 in-habitated revenue villages and 2358 hamlet villages. (Table 4.1.2).

TABLE 4.1.2: Anantapur District Administrative Profile.

Sl. No.	Item	Unit	
1.	Revenue Divisions	No	3
2.	Revenue Mandals	No	63
3.	Revenue Villages (Inhabitants)	No	964
4.	Hamlets	No	2358
5.	Total No. of Villages (Revenue Villages + Hamlets)	No	3322
6.	No. of Towns	No	10
7.	Gram Panchayats	No	1005
8.	Mandel Parishads	No	63

Source: 1. Hand Book of Anantapur District Statistics, Anantapur, 2002-03.
2. Census of India, 2001.

Population

Anantapur District is second largest district in Andhra Pradesh with a total area of 19130 sq.km. However the district is sparsely populated. **The density of population** of the District is only 190 persons per Sq.km., against (277) of the State. The population of rural and urban to the total population of the District works out to be 75 per cent and 25 per cent (2001 Census) as against 87.5 per cent of 1991 Census. There are 958 Females per 1000 Males (2001 Census).

The working force in the total population of District forms 48.83 per cent as per 2001 Census, out of which

26% are in the Agriculture Sector. The work participation rate for female is 39.4 and for male 57.8. Agriculture labour constitute main workforce (37.7 per cent). Agriculture labour is the mainstay for women workers (54.5) (Table 4.1.4).

TABLE 4.1.3: Population Characteristics of Anantapur District.

Sl. No.	Item	Unit	
1.	Density of Population	Per Sq.km	190
2.	Population	Lakhs	36.40
	Males	Lakhs	18.59
	Females	Lakhs	17.81
3.	Rural Population	Lakhs	27.21
4.	Urban Population	Lakhs	9.19
5.	Urban Population as % to Total	%	25.23
6.	Population of Scheduled Castes	%	14.14
7.	Population of Scheduled Tribes	%	3.5
8.	Population (0-6)		479853
9.	Sex-ratio	No	958
10.	Sex-ratio (0-6)	No	959
11.	Sex-ratio S.C.	No	956
12.	Sex-ratio S.T.	No	935
13.	No. of Households	No	779052
14.	Household size	No	5.0
15.	Literacy Rate		56.13
	Males		68.4
	Females		43.3
16.	Rural Literacy		44.63
17.	Urban Literacy		60.87

Source: 1. Hand Book of Anantapur District Statistics, Anantapur, 2002-03.
2. Census of India, 2001.

The district has low sex ratio, only 958 females per thousand males. It is further lower in the case of Scheduled Castes and Scheduled Tribe Population. The overall literacy rate in the district is only 56.13; and for rural areas it is much lower it is only 44.63 (see Table 4.1.3).

Table 4.1.4: Work Participation of Anantapur District

Sl. No.		Unit	Persons	Male	Female
1.	Total Workers	No	1777536	1075456	702080
2.	Proportion of Non-workers	%	51.2	42.2	60.6
3.	Main Workers	%	40.4	52.3	28.0
4.	Marginal Workers	%	8.4	5.6	11.4
5.	Proportion to Total Workers				
	Cultivators	%	29.8	32.3	25.9
	Agricultural Labour	%	37.7	26.8	54.5
	Household Industry	%	5.7	5.6	6.0
	Other Workers	%	26.7	35.3	13.6
6.	Work Participation Rate	%	48.8	57.8	39.4

Source: 1. Hand Book of Anantapur District Statistics, Anantapur, 2002-03.
2. Census of India, 2001.

Infrastructure

The details of communication, education and health services and infrastructure are shown in Tables 4.1.5 & 4.1.6. The district is provided with 8,702 kilometers length of road facility. However, 42.65 per cent only are connected with main road. 58.70 per cent of villages have bus stop facility. As many as 80.46 per cent village have primary schools. Only 13.58 per cent of villages have medical facilities within the village.

Table 4.1.5: Infrastructure.

Sl. No.	Item	Unit	
1.	Government Hospitals	No	93
2.	Villages electrification	No	933
3.	Degree colleges	No	38
4.	Jr. Colleges	No	100
5.	Schools (Including Primary, Upper Primary and High Schools)	No	4408

Source: 1. Hand Book of Anantapur District Statistics, Anantapur, 2002-03.
2. Census of India, 2001.

Table 4.1.6: Medical and Public Health.

Sl. No.	ITEM	YEAR		
		2000-01	2001-02	2002-03
1	2	3	4	5
I	Allopathic:			
	A. General Hospitals	14	14	14
	B. Hospitals for Special Treatment			
	(Specify)			
	i. C.D. Hospital, Anantapur	01	01	01
	ii. P.A.C. Dispensary, Anantapur	01	01	01
	iii. Police Hospital, Anantapur	01	01	01
	iv. Primary Health Centres	68	68	68
	C. Dispensaries	08	08	08
	D. (i) Beds	1394	1394	1394
	(ii) Beds (Lakh of Population)	38.30	37.5	37.17
	E. (i) Doctors	186	203	320
	(ii) Doctors per Lakh of Population	5.11	5.46	8.53

Contd....

1	2	3	4	5
II	Ayurvedic:			
	A. Hospitals	29	29	29
	B. Dispensaries	29	29	29
	C. Doctors/Vaids	29	29	29
III	Unani:			
	A. Hospitals & Dispensaries	13	13	13
	B. Doctors/tabeebs	13	13	13
IV	Homeopathy:			
	A. Hospitals & Dispensaries	12	12	12
	B. Doctors	12	12	12

Note: Information should relate to Government bodies including Municipalities, Zilla Parishads and Mandal Parishads.

Source: 1. Hand Book of Anantapur District Statistics, Anantapur, 2002-03.
2. Census of India, 2001.

SECTION II

Profile of Study Villages and Mandals

The present study is carried out in 19 villages spread in five revenue Mandals of the District. Of the 19 villages selected for the study, six villages are revenue villages and 13 villages are hamlet villages. The population size of these villages ranges from 106 persons to 1600 persons. Most of these villages are located in remote part of the district. They are partly bilinguinal villages. They are proximate to Karnataka State. The details of nature of villages are shown in Table 4.2.1. To present a clear picture of the study villages, the background characteristics of the revenue Mandals from which study villages are drawn is explained in the following pages.

The study villages represent five revenue mandals. They are Agali, Amarapuram, Gudibanda, Madakasira and Rolla

Table 4.1.7: Communication, Education and Medical Facilities in the Villages of Anantapur District

Facility Item within the Village	Total No. of Inhabitated villages	No. of Villages having the facility	No. of Villages not having the Facility by Distance		
			0 -2km	2 – 5km	5km & above
Medical Facility	3322	451	784	1115	972
Primary School	3322	2673	513	71	19
Upper Primary School	3322	511	1046	987	699
Main Road	3322	1417	933	736	230
Bus Stop	3322	1950	808	481	73

Source: 1. Hand Book of Anantapur District Statistics, Anantapur, 2002-03.
2. Census of India, 2001.

Mandals. These mandals are located in remote and isolate part of the District. They are relatively small in area and are more backward mandals.

The distinctive feature of these mandals is that they have more number of hamlet villages than the revenue villages. 78.86 per cent of the villages in these mandals have less than 2000 population. 14.51 per cent of the villages have less than 200 persons. These details are presented in Table 4.2.2. None of these mandals have urban centres and thus there is no urban population.

The density of population in the mandals under reference however, is higher than the district average. Only Madakasira Mandal has lesser density than District. The Scheduled Caste Population is more than 20 per cent to total population in these Mandals. The Scheduled Caste population concentration thus is more by six per cent than the District. The Scheduled Tribe Population constitutes less than two per cent in these mandals. This distribution is lesser than the District level composition.

The mandals under reference have relatively better sex-ratio than the district average sex-ratio. But the female literacy is lower than the district average.

The work participation rate is higher than the District. The work participation rate of the District is 48.8 per cent whereas in all the mandals under reference the work participation rate ranges between 51.2 to 55.8. The women work participation rate is also rather high in mandals under reference. Female work participation rate in the District is 39.4. Whereas the female work participation rate in the mandals under reference ranges between 44.0 to 50.9. Agriculture labour is the major work activity for both male and female. The percentage of marginal workers is also higher than district average for both male and females. These details are presented in Table 4.2.3.

Table 4.2.1: Villages under Study by Revenue Mandal.

Name of the Mandal	No. of Rev. Villages	No. of Hamlets in the Mandal	Revenue Village	No. of Hamlets	Selected Village		Population
1	2	3	4	5	6		7
Agali	9	51	Hulikeradevara Halli	4	1.	Hulikeradevara Halli	555
			Kodi Halli	9	2.	Ragalingana Halli	1031
Gudibanda	13	16	Gudibanda	10	3.	P.G. Halli	148
					4.	Phalaram	223
			Ralla palli	7	5.	Ralapalli	1408
					6.	Mynagana Palli	712
					7.	Keynchayyan Palyam	106
Madakasira	20	97	Madakasira	8	8.	A. Golla Hatti	377
					9.	Chipulati	882
					10.	Vadra Palyam	357
			Govindapuram	13	11.	E. Golla Hatti	224

1	2	3	4	5	6		7
			Gowdan Halli	3	12.	Gowdan Halli	1507
					13.	Jamman palli	527
Amarapuram	9	46	Valasa	4	14.	Valasa	2201
			Thammala Palli	4	15.	Thammalapalli	1563
			Hemavathi	7	16.	Gollamaram hatti	706
Rolla	7	57	Rolla	17	17.	Rolla	1691
					18.	Kallurappam gollahatti	407
					19.	Pala Gollahatti	346

Source: 1. Hand Book of Anantapur District Statistics, Anantapur, 2002-03.
2. Census of India, 2001.

Table 4.2.2: Profile of Study Revenue Mandals.

Sl. No.		Unit	Agali	Amara-puram	Gudibanda	Madak-asira	Rolla	Anantapur Dist.
1.	No. of Revenue Villages	No	7	8	13	19	7	964
2.	No. of Villages	No	45	38	49	77	71	3322
3.	Population (Persons)	No	31886	52717	47838	73222	34888	36.40 (lakhs)
4.	0-6 Population	No	4042	7136	6454	9709	4626	479853
5.	Proportion of Urban Population	%	0.0	0.0	0.0	0.0	0.0	25.3
6.	Schedule Caste Population	%	21.0	22.0	23.6	22.3	20.1	25.3
7.	Scheduled Tribe Population	%	0.6	0.8	2.0	3.2	1.5	3.5
8.	Sex-ratio	No	976	963	952	961	990	958
9.	Sex-ratio (0-6)	No	937	948	968	954	1026	959
10.	S.C. Sex-ratio	No	946	975	953	960	987	956
11.	S.T. Sex-ratio	No	809	861	854	917	965	935
12.	Household Size	No	5.0	5.0	5.0	5.0	5.0	5.0
13.	Literacy Rate – Persons	%	54.6	50.9	47.8	53.7	51.5	56.1
	Males	%	97.0	63.2	60.5	66.8	63.6	68.4
	Females	%	41.9	38.1	34.4	40.2	39.2	43.4
14.	Density		220	217	214	187	213	190
15.	Area		139.6	242.6	223.9	391.2	163.7	19130

Source: 1. Hand Book of Anantapur District Statistics, Anantapur, 2002-03.
2. Census of India, 2001.

COMMUNICATION, EDUCATION AND HEALTH FACILITIES

The total number of habitations (Villages) in the five Revenue Mandals under reference is 332. The availability of communication (Bus Stop and Main Road), primary school, upper primary school and medical facilities within the village as well as their proximate distance of availability are presented in Tables 4.2.4 to 4.2.8.

Of the 332 villages of these five mandals only 44.58 per cent of the villages have bus stop facility within the village. 32 per cent of the villages however have a bus stop at a distance of more than 2 kilometers. Similarly 44.57 per cent of villages do not have facility of main road. 30 per cent of the villages have to treck more than two kilometers to avail main approach.

Only 73.91 per cent of the villages have facility of primary school within village. Children of the 6.55 per cent of the villages have to slog more than two kilometers to avail primary school education. The situation is primarily due to the small size habitations. Only 10.24 per cent of the villages have the facility of upper primary school. Children of 50.75 per cent of the villages have to walk more than two kilometers to avail upper primary education.

Only 8.43 of the villages have medical facility within the village. 31.32 per cent however can avail medical facility within 2 kilometers radious. 70.48 per cent of the villages have drinking water facility arranged by Rural Water Supply Scheme. 29.5 per cent of the villages depend on bore-wells for drinking water. The above details are however notwithstanding the intra-mandal village variations. The actual situation can be much harsher than the statistical profile.

Table 4.2.3: Mandal-wise Habitations According to Population.

Name of the Mandal	No. of Habitations	<200	200-2000	2000-4000	4000-6000	8000	10000>	Total
Madakasira	97	19(6.00)	76(23.97)	1(0.31)	0	0	1(0.31)	97(30.60)
Gudibanda	66	12(3.79)	52(16.40)	2(0.63)	0	0	0	66(20.82)
Amarapuram	46	8(2.52)	33(10.41)	4(1.26)	0	1(0.31)	0	46(14.51)
Agali	51	8(2.52)	41(12.93)	2(0.63)	0	0	0	51(16.09)
Rolla	57	9(2.83)	48(15.14)	0	0	0	0	57(17.98)
Total	**317**	**46(14.51)**	**250(78.86)**	**9(2.84)**	**0**	**1(0.31)**	**1(0.31)**	**317**

Source: 1. Hand Book of Anantapur District Statistics, Anantapur, 2002-03.
2. Census of India, 2001.

SECTION III

SOCIO-ECONOMIC STATUS OF THE RESPONDENTS

In this Section an attempt is made to examine the socio-economic status of the respondents the first objective of the present. Our study sample comprises a total of 229 subjects drawn from 19 villages and represent such caste communities as Adavi Golla, Boya, Madiga and Mala Communities. These communities belong to backward caste and scheduled castes categories. The socio-economic status is examined with reference to socio-cultural, demographic and economic indicators. The independent variable is caste.

THE SOCIO-CULTURAL STATUS

The socio-cultural status is examined with reference to caste status, religious status, type of family and educational status. The study is based on 229 respondents. All the respondents belong to Hindu religion. They represent Madiga (27.5 per cent), Mala (2.6 per cent), Boya (26.2 per cent) and Adavi Golla (43.7 per cent) caste communities. Mala and Madiga belong to Scheduled Castes. Boya and Adavi Golla represent Backward Class Communities. The ethnographic details of these communities are presented in following pages.

ADAVI GOLLA

Adavi Gollas are a backward community. They are listed as backward class category D in Andhra Pradesh. Adavi Gollas are a sub-sect of Golla community. The Adavi Gollas are considered to be archaic in beliefs and practices. They are spread mostly in the erstwhile Madakasira Taluq and in neighbouring State of Karnataka.

Table 4.2 4: Work Participation of Study Revenue Mandals.

Sl. No.			Unit	Agali	Amara-puram	Gudibanda	Madak-asira	Rolla	Anantapur Dist.
1.	Non-workers	Persons	%	44.2	47.7	47.4	48.8	45.0	51.2
		Females	%	49.1	54.3	52.8	56.0	50.6	60.6
2.	Main Workers	Persons	%	39.8	39.4	38.1	43.8	40.1	40.4
		Females	%	28.8	27.9	27.1	33.6	29.4	28.0
3.	Marginal Workers	Persons	%	16.1	12.9	14.5	7.4	14.9	8.4
		Females	%	22.2	17.8	20.1	10.3	20.0	11.4
4.	Proportion of Total Workers Cultivators	Persons	%	35.8	38.4	42.2	34.5	40.8	29.8
		Females	%	20.1	27.9	32.0	28.1	29.7	25.9
5.	Agricultural Labours	Persons	%	44.5	41.9	42.0	46.0	39.1	37.7
		Females	%	60.7	56.5	57.4	62.0	52.2	54.5
6.	Household Industry	Persons	%	8.5	6.5	2.3	1.5	5.7	5.7
		Females	%	13.0	9.3	3.3	1.9	9.7	6.0
7.	Other Workers	Persons	%	11.2	13.2	13.5	18.1	14.3	26.7
		Females	%	6.3	6.4	7.3	8.0	8.4	13.6
8.	Work Participation Rate	Persons	%	55.8	52.3	52.6	51.2	55.0	48.8
		Females	%	50.9	45.7	47.2	44.0	49.4	39.4

Source: 1. Hand Book of Anantapur District Statistics, Anantapur, 2002-03.
2. Census of India, 2001.

Table 4.2.5: Communication Facility in Mandals under Study.

Name of the Mandal	Total Inhabited Villages (No.)	Villages having Bus Stop Facility	Villages not having a Bus Stop According to Distance from Nearest Bus Stop (No.)		
			Less than 2 k.m.s.	2 to 5 k.m.s.	5 k.m.s. & above
Madakasira	100	43	16	25	16
Amarapuram	48	20	17	11	0
Gudibanda	67	32	15	20	0
Rolla	63	32	18	13	0
Agali	54	21	12	17	4
Total	332	148 (44.58)	78 (23.50)	86 (25.90)	20 (6.02)
District	3322	1950 (58.70)	808 (24.32)	481 (14.48)	73 (2.18)

Source: 1. Hand Book of Anantapur District Statistics, Anantapur, 2002-03.
2. Census of India, 2001.

Table 4.2.6: Main Road Facility in Mandals under Study.

Name of the Mandal	Total Inhabited Villages (no.)	Villages having Bus Stop Facility	Villages not on Main Road According to Distance from Main Road		
			Less than 2 k.m.s.	2 to 5 k.m.s.	5 k.m.s. & above
Madakasira	100	43	16	25	16
Amarapuram	48	20	17	11	0
Gudibanda	67	32	19	16	0
Rolla	63	32	18	13	0
Agali	54	21	12	17	4
Total	332	148 (44.58)	82 (24.70)	82 (24.70)	20 (6.02)
District	3322	1417 (42.66)	933 (28.09)	736 (22.16)	230 (6.92)

Source: 1. Hand Book of Anantapur District Statistics, Anantapur, 2002-03.
2. Census of India, 2001.

Table 4.2.7: Primary & Upper Primary School Facility in the Villages.

Name of the Mandal	Habited Villages (No.)	Having Primary School (No.)	To Distance from Primary School (no.)			Having Upper Primary School (No.)	According to Distance from Upper Primary School (No.)		
			Less than 2 k.m.s.	2 to 5 k.m.s.	5 k.m.s. &Above		Less than 2 k.m.s.	2 to 5 k.m.s.	5 k.m.s. & Above
Madakasira	100	43	36	6	15	8	41	26	25
Amarapuram	48	44	4	0	0	3	19	17	2
Gudibanda	67	58	3	0	0	6	14	32	15
Rolla	63	55	0	0	0	9	24	24	6
Agali	54	38	8	0	0	8	30	16	0
Total	332 (73.91)	238 (15.84)	51 (1.86)	6 (4.66)	15 (10.24)	34 (38.55)	128 (34.64)	115 (14.46)	48
District	3322 (80.46)	2673 (15.44)	513 (2.14)	71 (0.57)	19 (0.63)	511 (31.49)	1046 (29.71)	987 (21.04)	699

Source: 1. Hand Book of Anantapur District Statistics, Anantapur, 2002-03.
2. Census of India, 2001.

Table 4.2.8: Medical Facility in Mandals under Study.

Name of the Mandal	Total Inhabited Villages (No.)	Villages having Medical Facility (Govt. Only)	Villages not having Medical Facility According to Distance from Nearest Place having it (No.)		
			Less than 2k.ms	2 to 5 k.ms	5 kms. & above
Madakasira	100	2	46	26	26
Amarapuram	48	5	21	18	4
Gudibanda	67	8	18	19	22
Rolla	63	7	25	15	16
Agali	54	6	22	26	0
Total	332 (%)	28 (8.43)	132 (39.76)	104 (31.32)	68 (20.48)
District	3322	451 (13.58)	784 (23.60)	1115 (33.56)	972 (29.26)

Source: 1. Hand Book of Anantapur District Statistics, Anantapur, 2002-03.
2. Census of India, 2001.

Table 4.2.9: Adequate Drinking Water Facility in Mandals Under Study.

Name of the Mandal	Total Inhabited Villages (No.)	Villages having Adequate Drinking Water Facility (No.)				Problematic villages (no.)		
		PWS	Bore-wells	Open wells	Others	Fluoride Villages	Brakish Water	Not having Drinking Water Facility
Madakasira	100	39	61	-	-	-	-	-
Amarapuram	48	44	4	-	-	-	-	-
Gudibanda	67	62	5	-	-	42	-	-
Rolla	63	48	15	-	-	8	-	-
Agali	54	41	13	-	-	12	-	-
Total	332 (%)	234	98					
		70.48	29.52					
District	3322	2093	1198	25	133	866	37	-
		63.00	36.06	0.75	4.00	26.07	1.11	

Source: 1. Hand Book of Anantapur District Statistics, Anantapur, 2002-03.
2. Census of India, 2001.

Golla/Gulla also known as Yadava, Handi Golla, Advi Golla or Gopala. The Golla/Gulla Derive their community name from the Sanskrit word gopala, meaning protector of cows. Thurston (1909), describes the Golla of Madras Presidency as a pastoral caste who tend sheep, goat and cattle and sell milk.

Thurston (1909), has identified some sub-divisions, such as Pakanti (eastern territory), Gauda or Gaudu (cowherds), Kadu or Kattu (forest), Konar, Erra (red), Peddenti (beggar), Astaandra, Musti (exorcist), Puja, Puni, Karna, Racha or Rachu (royal), Uru and Bokkisa. Each sub-division is, in turn, divided into clans, of which the sixteen that have been identified are Avulu (vow), Chintala (tamarind), Gurram (horse), Nakka or Nakkala (jackal), Katari (dagger), Kokala (woman's sari), Mugi, (dumb), Mekala (goats), Chettula (trees), Chevvula (ears), Gorrela, (Sheep), Gorantla (Lawsonia albatenna), Puli (tiger), Raghindala (papal), Saddikudu (cold rice or food) and Mushtiga.

Hassan (1920), states that Gulla, Gullai, Gollwar, Gavali and Dhangar were the synonyms of the Golla, a pastoral caste found in the erstwhile Telugu and Carnatic Districts.

According to Ananthakrishna Iyer (1930), the Golla of Mysore was engaged in tending cattle and selling milk and milk products. Their two divisions, namely Onti-Chapparamuvulu and Rendu-Chapparamuvallu, are each further divided into several endogamous divisions, namely Yerra or Kilari Golla, Punagu or Kudi-paitala Golla, Kanne Golla, Puni or Piye Golla Bigamudre or Bokkasa Golla, Kanchu Golla, Racha Golla and Musti Golla. They have about sixty clans. They are non-vegetarian, and rice and ragi constitute their staple cereals.

The Golla have two sub-groups, Kadu Golla or Adavi Golla, meaning those who live in forests and Uru Golla, meaning those who live in villages. The community has patrilineal clans, such as Kardi, Sannar, Kengori, Ainer and Kondnar, which are exogamous.

Marriage is permitted with one's father's sister's daughter, mother's brother's daughter or elder sister's daughter. Vermilion, thali and toe-rings are the symbols of marriage. Bride-price (tera) is a prevalent and practice. Divorce is allowed and remarriage is practiced. All male children are given equal shares in the family property, while the right of succession is held by the eldest son.

Women take part in agricultural operations and animal husbandry. Some important life-cycle rituals performed include a pre-delivery ritual (Basiru adiqe) in the seventh month of pregnancy, the naming ceremony (namakarana) within forry days of childbirth, and puberty rites for girls (hosige). They practice burial and observe pollution (suthka) for eleven days.

The traditional as well as present-day occupation of the Golla is rearing sheep and goats. Largely landless, a small number of them work in government service and as agricultural daily-wage labourers. The Golla's community council is fined or social boycotted. At the regional level, they have an association called Yadava Sangha which works for community welfare.

Their deities include Chittalingeshwar, Gollama and Maramma. They invite a Brahman priest to officiate at the marriage ceremony.

They accept water and cooked food from the Brahman, Lingayat and Satani Communities, and exchange the same with the Kuruba and Nayaka but not with the Adi Dravida and Adi Karnataka. However, sidha food is exchanged with all. Water sources, burial grounds and religious shrines are shared with other Hindu communities.

By and large Loan facilities extended by the IRDP and others agencies for buying sheep and goats are utilized by them. Some of them are self-employed in animal husbandry and petty business.

BOYA

Boyas are one of the numerically large caste communities spread in Anantapur District. Boyas belong to de-notified tribes (Vimukta Jati). They are included in backward class category-A in State of Andhra Pradesh. However, in Agency areas of Andhra Pradesh and as well as in neighbouring Karnataka State they are listed as Scheduled Tribe.

Synonymously known as Kirathaka, Nayakudu, Sabari, Nishad, Talari, Valimiki etc., the Boya are spread throughout Andhra Pradesh but their larger concentration is in the Kurnool, Anantapur, Cuddapah and Guntur Districts. They are known to have been specifically engaged in carrying umbrellas and palankin during the reign of the Vijayanagara Rules. The Boya speak Telugu and use the Telugu script.

The traditional occupation of the Boya was hunting. They were also known to be involved in dacoit, way side robbery, umbrella and palankin bearers. They ware also known to be warriors and were involved in martial activities. A few of Boyas also have become Palegars (Local Chieftan) in the past as reward to their warrior activities. At present, the majority of them are agricultural labourers, while a few are cultivators and very few in the other services.

Based on occupational differentiation, the Boya have two groups, namely Pedda Boys and Chinna Boya. Inter-marriages do not take place between the two. A few of their surnames are Mallabothula, Jampala, Kandi, Gujjala Meenigela and Ujjala. Cross-cousin and maternal uncle-nice marriages are preferred. Divorce is permissible. A widow can live with any man of the community and beget children and they are considered as legal heirs. The Boya observe the naming, mundane and annaprashan ceremonies and puberty rites. The wedding ceremonies comprise the engagement, reception of the bridegroom's, exchange of garlands, sprinkling of sacred rice over the bridal couple, typing of the thali, etc. The dead are buried and pollution and rituals like China and Pedda Dinalu are observed.

The AIBAS data shows that the average household size of the Boya of Andhra Pradesh is five, and males constitute 52 per cent of the total population. Unmarried males are more (54 per cent) than unmarried females (34 per cent), while the percentage of widows is high (12 per cent). The Boya are non-vegetarian; rice; ragi and Jowar are their staple cereals.

A Brahman priest is consulted for fixing an auspicious day and time for marriage but he does not officiate at the marriage ceremonies. The Boya accept water and food from other communities but do not maintain commensal relations with the Mala and Madiga. They share wells, crematoria and religious shrines with others.

Some of the education among them is teachers, doctors, engineers, etc., the literacy level of the Boya is low on account of socio-economic constraints. The attitude of the Boya towards family planning is favourable but couples normally prefer three children. The facilities of drinking water, transport, communication and self-employment programme are utilized by them.

The Boya's state-level association, the Valmiki Seva Sangham, was formed in 1929.

MADIGA

The Madiga caste community is listed as scheduled caste community in Andhra Pradesh. This community is one of the numerically largest communities among scheduled caste of Andhra Pradesh. Among the scheduled castes of Anantapur District Madigas are considered to be numerically largest and are spread throughout. The Madiga are distributed in Karnataka, Andhra Pradesh, Tamil Nadu, Kerala and Maharashtra.

According to the 1981 census, the population of the Madiga in Andhra Pradesh is 3,572,072. They live predominantly in the rural areas. Telugu is their mother tongue and they use the Telugu script.

The Madiga of Andhra Pradesh are also referred to as Adi Andhra, Arundhatiya, Jambavalu, etc. They prefer to use the terms, Adi Andhra, Adi Karnataka, Adi Dravida, etc., and believes that they represent the original substratum of the people in the land.

Stories prevalent among the people about their ancestors such as Matangia (a Sanskrit name for goddess Kali) and Jambava (who was associated with the armies of the allies of Rama) are mentioned by them. The Madiga (SC) of Maharastra explains that the word, Madiga is derived from mahadiga, meaning a greatman who came down. This is usually substantiated by relating a story which traces their origin from Jambuvanth, the bear-beaded man referred to in the epic Ramayana. The Madiga and the Mala have common legends that speak of their origins. Many legends say that the divine cow, Kamadhenu, was killed by two watchmen of Eeswara and as a consequence they were cursed by Him. The descendants of these two watchmen are the Madiga and Mala.

Nanjuddayya and Iyer (1931), state, 'the Madiga who are also known as left-hand caste or Edagaiyavaru, among themselves ... apply the term Jambavas, Padmajatiyavaru and Matanagas.

The traditional occupation of the Madiga is leather-work and making footwear. Most of them also work as agricultural labourers. Their traditional and present-day occupations also include scavenging, village servants and drum-beaters. Whereas in the urban centres many of them have taken up industrial work.

Very few of them own land. Those who have small landholdings also work as agricultural labourers. Agricultural labourers on an annual contract are paid in grain. They purchase leather and other materials needed for shoe-making and footwear. Their women assist in the tanning of hides and also act as midwives.

Ananda Row (1901)*, identifies two endogamous sub-divisions, the Desabhanga and the others, among the Madiga. As quoted in Thurston (1909), the Desabhanga are further divided into six sub-classes, namely Billoru (bowmen), Malloru (mallu meaning fight), Amaravatiyavaru (called after a town), Munigolu (muni or rishi), Yenamaloru (buffalo) and Movabuvvadavaru (those who place food in a winnow). Among the Telugu section of the Madiga, various surnames (intiperu), which are in fact lineages, serve as exogamous groups.

There are many sub-divisions among the Madiga, such as Gampa Domati, Chela Domati, Unnam and Daruluri are their surnames. Hassan (1920), states that the Madiga are leather-workers, rope-makers and also serve as servants. Appa, Ayy and Amma titles are accorded to them. He mentions two divisions among them, namely Canara Madiga and Telugu Madiga, 25 sub-tribes and nine territorial divisions. Kumollu (horn), Andyarollu (castor plant), Gatollu (hill), Katkoorollu (sword), Gaddapollu (beard) and Awalollu (cow) among them. They observe surname (intiperu) exogamy. The Madiga Dasu officiate as priests for all life-cycle rituals.

The AIBAS data shows that the average household size of the Madiga of Andhra Pradesh is six and the ratio of males (50 per cent) and females (49 per cent) is almost equal in the total population. Married females (57 per cent) are relatively more in comparison to married males (53 per cent) while the percentage of widowed females is 8. The Madiga are non-vegetarian and frequently consume alcoholic drinks. Community councils (Kulapanchayat) which were common till recently have become defunct.

They are Hindu by faith and mainly worship Lord Shiva and Lord Vishnu. Their caste deities are Matangi (Durga) and Ellamma. Many of them have embraced Christianity. Their social interaction with other communities in the village is limited, but in urban areas, many of the Madiga are able to secure good jobs by virtue of their education. They have responded favourably to various developmental activities and realize that these programmes have helped change their lives. Their literacy rate, according to the 1981 census, is only 11.31 per cent.

They have a specific duty of beating the drums during all fairs (thirunallu) and in funeral processions.

Their literacy rate, according to the 1981 census, is 27.76 per cent. They have availed themselves of loans for self-employment from the banks and with financial assistance have given their traditional occupation a boost.

MALA

Malas belong Scheduled Castes. Mala also referred to as Adi-Andhra. In the earlier decennial reports they have been mentioned as Arundatiya and Jambavulu, but these names actually refer to the Madiga. Hassan (1920), notes that they were known to the Mohammedans by the name Dher. Antyaja and Panchama were the other synonyms reported. They are mainly concentrated in Andhra Pradesh but are also returned from Tamil Nadu, Pondicherry, Karnataka and Maharashtra. They also live in Madhya Pradesh were they are not notified as a scheduled caste.

In Andhra Pradesh the Mala are distributed in all districts. According to a Telugu legend, Lord Shiva's two watchmen connived with each other and killed the divine cow, Kammadhenu. They were later found guilty and were cursed by the lord to be born as menial servants. Thus, the two watchmen, Mala and Madiga, and their descendants have become two menial castes. The Mala have Rampala, Murikinati, Dayininda, Turasana, Kannada, Koyi and Rohini. Their mother tongue is Telugu. In the border areas of Maharashtra, Karnataka and Tamil Nadu they also speak Marathi, Kannada and Tamil, respectively. Their total population, according 1981 census, is 2,896,642. The AIAS data (1st Phase) on the Mala of Andhra Pradesh shows that they are on average below medium in stature with an average of 163 cm. they have a long headed with medium nose and broad medium face. It appears from the AIBAS data that the average household size of the Mala of Andhra Pradesh is five males constitute 53 per cent of the total population. Married females are relatively more (55 per cent) in comparison to married males (48 per cent). Serogenetic studies of the Mala from Hyderabad and Warngal Districts indicate that unlike the Proto-Australoid tribal groups of these areas they have an excess of gene B, as compared with the average level in the state. They also have a low incidence (2.7 per cent) of Hp^2 while gene E & D2 is found in 36.4 per cent (Rami Reddy et al., 1980). The morphometric variation of the Mala of different areas in the state show a greater variation, suggesting the existence of breeding isolates within the Mala. They are non-vegetarian. They smoke an indigenous cheroot (Chutta), particularly their women who keep the burning end in the mouth. However, smoking of chutta is on the wane.

NATURE OF FAMILY

Nuclear families predominate among the respondents. Majority of the respondents under reference belong to nuclear families (71.6 per cent). Only 28.4 per cent respondents belong to joint families. The data indicates that the nature of family in rural areas has under gone a radical change from joint family to nuclear family. Joint families are found to be more among Mala Community (50.00 per cent) and Boya Community (36.66 per cent) followed by Madiga (25.39 per cent) and Adavi Golla (24.00 per cent) communities.

LITERACY

The respondents are characterized by poor literacy levels. Our data reveals that illiteracy among the respondents under reference is rather high (62.8 per cent). The data indicates that this percentage is much higher than the average district percentage of female illiteracy which is 59.1. The illiteracy is found to be highest among Adavi Golla members (74.00 per cent) followed by Madiga community members (61.90 per cent), Mala members 50.00 per cent and Boya women 43.33 per cent. Only 12.7 per cent of the respondents have studies above S.S.C level. In other words these members have more 10 years of education.

More specifically among Madiga women members, only 9.52 per cent obtained about 10 years of education; among Mala females it was 33.33 per cent and among Boya women 28.3 per cent have more 10 years of education. Only 4.00 per cent of Adavi Golla women have received more than 10 years of Education. The details of levels of education are presented in Table 4.3.1.

Table 4.3.1: Distribution of Respondents Levels of Education and Caste.

Education	Caste				Total
	Madiga	Mala	Adavi Golla	Boya	
Illiterate	39 (61.9)	3 (50.0)	74 (74.0)	26 (43.3)	142 (62.0)
literate	5 (7.9)	0 (0.0)	5 (5.0)	5 (8.3)	15 (6.6)
Primary	3 (4.8)	0 (0.0)	11 (11.0)	8 (13.3)	22 (9.6)
S.S.C.	9 (14.3)	1 (16.7)	6 (6.0)	4 (6.7)	20 (8.7)
S.S.C. above	6 (9.5)	2 (33.3)	4 (4.0)	17 (28.3)	29 (12.7)
Not Applicable	1 (1.6)	0 (0.0)	0 (0.0)	0 (0.0)	1 (0.4)
Total	63 (100.0)	6 (100.0)	100 (100.0)	60 (100.0)	229 (100.0)

DEMOGRAPHIC FEATURES

The demographic features are examined with reference to marital status, age and size of the family of the respondents.

All the 229 respondents under reference are women and they are married. The average age of the respondents under study is found to be 31.41 years. Caste-wise Mala women are older in age (32.50 years). The average age of Adavi Golla and Madiga caste women is found to be 31.69 and 31.62 years respectively. The average age of Boya women is found to be 30.60 years.

However, 28.8 per cent of respondents belong to the age group of 15 to 25 years. Only 5.7 per cent of women under reference are aged above 46 years. Among the Madiga Community 31.74 per cent are aged between 15 to 25 years. Among Adavi Golla Community 29.00 per cent are age between 15 to 25 years. 26.66 per cent of Boya women and 16.6 per cent of Mala women are less than 25 years age. The age distribution of respondents is presented in Table 4.3.2.

Table 4.3.2: Distribution of Respondents of Age and Caste.

Education	Caste				Total
	Madiga	Mala	Adavi Golla	Boya	
15 - 25	20 (31.7)	1 (16.7)	29 (29.0)	16 (26.7)	66 (28.8)
26 - 35	28 (44.4)	4 (66.7)	44 (44.0)	29 (48.3)	105 (45.9)
36 -45	10 (15.9)	1 (16.7)	19 (19.0)	15 (25.0)	45 (19.7)
46>	5 (7.9)	0 (0.0)	8 (8.0)	0 (0.0)	13 (5.7)
Total	63 (100.0)	6 (100.0)	100 (100.0)	60 (100.0)	229 (100.0)

SIZE OF FAMILY

The respondent's size of family varies from two members to 15 members. The mean average size of the family is found to be 4.76 members. This is lower than the district average size of the household (5 members). 36.2 per cent of the respondent's family size is found to be four members only. However, 5.1 per cent of the respondent's families consist of more than eight members. Such families are found to be more in Adavi Golla and Boya Communities. 14.4 per cent of households understudy comprise three and less number of members. Such families are found to be more in Madiga Community. These details are presented in Table 4.3.3.

Table 4.3.3: Number of Persons in the Family by Caste.

No. of Persons	Caste				Total
	Madiga	Mala	Adavi Golla	Boya	
2	6 (9.5)	0 (0.0)	4 (4.0)	1 (1.7)	11 (4.8)
3	7 (11.1)	0 (0.0)	8 (8.0)	7 (11.7)	22 (9.6)
4	25 (39.7)	1 (16.7)	38 (38.0)	19 (31.7)	83 (36.2)
5	16 (25.4)	2 (33.3)	24 (24.0)	16 (26.7)	58 (25.3)
6	7 (11.1)	2 (33.3)	14 (14.0)	10 (16.7)	33 (14.4)
7	1 (1.6)	0 (0.0)	4 (4.0)	5 (8.3)	10 (4.4)
8	1 (1.6)	0 (0.0)	3 (3.0)	0 (0.0)	4 (1.7)
9	0 (0.0)	1 (16.7)	3 (3.0)	2 (3.3)	6 (2.6)
10	0 (0.0)	0 (0.0)	1 (1.0)	0 (0.0)	1 (0.4)
15	0 (0.0)	0 (0.0)	1 (1.0)	0 (0.0)	1 (0.4)
Total	63 (100.0)	6 (100.0)	100 (100.0)	60 (100.0)	229 (100.0)

ECONOMIC STATUS

The economic status is examined with reference to annual income, occupation and land holdings of the respondents. The respondent's annual income ranges from a minimum of Rs.5000 to a maximum of Rs. 18000

women in the richest quintile than those in the poorest in sub-Saharan Africa, and eight times higher in South Asia (Greene, 2005).

Hemminki (1997), also noted that Access to care and the experience of treatment are also difficult among women in the lower socioeconomic status (Hemminki, 1997). Similarly, Molesworth, K. (2005), observed that poor communications and transport infrastructure can be important in preventing access to services in rural areas, especially in maternal health care where transport to referral services is an essential component of dealing with emergencies and preventing mortality (Molesworth, 2005).

Another major factor contributing to unequal access to services is stigma and marginalization. People with alternative sexual identities, or who in some way do not conform to societal norms, face stigma, discrimination and violence, often backed up by repressive laws. This can limit their access to services, for example for fear of persecution or abuse, or by pushing groups underground so that it is hard to access them with programmes (Berger, 2005).

Many studies have documented how traditional practices and beliefs also affect access to services. For example, in many countries it is standard practice to seek the services of traditional healers over public health service providers, in particular for SRH issues; a study in India found that many pregnant women preferred services of a lay attendant to those of a midwife (Matthews, 2005).

In view of above reflections it is pertinent to analyze these factors. Hence, our second objective of the study is to analyze the access to communication, Education, and Medical and Health Facilities.

The communication facility is analyzed with reference to the availability of bus stop. The education facility is examined with reference to availability of Primary School,

High school and Junior College. The medical facility is examined with reference to the availability of Health Sub-centre, Primary Health Centre, Govt. Hospital and Govt. Medical Facility, Angnawadi and Private Medical Facility. Health care facility is examined with reference to availability of health professional such as ANM/Nurse, Health Worker/ TBA and Doctor (Allopathy).

COMMUNICATION

Connectivity to the majority of the rural areas in Anantapur District is provided by public road transport system through buses. Therefore the availability of bus stop is an important indicator for not only communication but also for accessing health care facilities.

Our data reveals that a large percentage of villages and thereby the respondents (56.8 per cent) have the bus stop facility within their village. 29.7 per cent of the respondents have the facility of bus stop at distance of less than two kilometers. 4.4 per cent of the respondents have to trek beyond six kilometers to avail their bus facility. 9.2 per cent of the respondents have access to bus stop facility at distance of 3-5 kilometers.

Thus, our data shows that a seizable percentage (43.2 per cent) of respondents do not have access to facility of bus stop and thus are excluded from communication means of cheap, affordable motor transport to avail medical and health facilities, in case of need. More specifically 48.0 per cent and 33.3 per cent of Adavi Golla and Boya members respectively have to trek up to two kilometers to avail the bus facility. 21.0 per cent of Adavi Golla members and 15.9 per cent of Madiga members have to go more than three kilometers to avail the public transport system.

EDUCATIONAL FACILITIES

The access to Primary School facility within the village is being enjoyed by 86.5 per cent to avail primary schooling facility. For the remaining 13.5 per cent the school is within two kilometers reach. 17.5 per cent of Madiga members, 16.7 per cent of Boya members and ten per cent of Adavi Golla members experience this inconvenience.

With regard to access to High School Education the scenario is different. Completion of high school means ten years of schooling. 26.6 per cent have access to high school within the village. The high school is away by more than three kilometers for 17.0 per cent and more than six kilometers for 4.4 per cent of respondents. However, for a large majority (52.0 per cent) the high school is accessible within two kilometers. More specifically, 15.9 per cent Madiga members and 29.0 per cent of Adavi Golla members avail high school facility within five kilometers. Another 15.9 per cent of Madiga members however, go beyond five kilometers to avail high school facility.

ACCESS TO HEALTH PROFESSIONALS

An analysis of access to health professionals reveals that health professionals like Allopathy Doctor, ANM/Nurse, Health/Trained Birth Attendant, Anganwadi Worker and Private Doctor are the different health professional accessible to respondents. The details of accessibility to health professional and medical facilities is presented Table 4.4.1 A & B.

Our data shows that health worker/trained birth attendant is accessible within the village for 58.5 per cent of respondents. This is followed by the services of ANM/ Nurse whose services can be availed by 49.8 per cent of respondents within the village. Only 18.8 per cent respondents can have access to Doctor within the village.

The data further reveals that none of the Adavi Golla members can avail the services of doctor within the village. To avail the services of doctor these members have to go beyond three kilometers (40.0 per cent) and six kilometers (40.0). 46.0 per cent of Madiga members and 33.3 per cent of Boya members can avail the services of doctor within the village. The services of doctor are available at distance of more than six kilometers for Madiga (15.9 per cent) Boya (23.3 per cent) and Adavi Golla (40.0).

The Adavi Golla members experience difficulty in availing the services of even Health Worker/Trained Birth Attendant and ANM/Nurse. They are available at a distance of more than three kilometers for these members. Majority of the Scheduled Caste members can avail the services of these members either within the village or within the reach of three kilometers. All the Boya members can avail the services of these members within the village itself. Thus, our data shows that as far as accessibility to services of grass-root health professionals is concerned, Scheduled Castes experience is greater Social Inclusion and on the other hand Adavi Gollas experience Social Exclusion. The only exception however is Adavi Golla members. This is partly due to their habitation settlements.

MEDICAL FACILITY

Our data shows that government health facility can be availed by 13.1 per cent within the village; 34.9 per cent by at distance of within two kilometers and at distance of more than six kilometers by 34.5 per cent.

On the contrary private health facility can be availed within the village by 34.5 per cent and within a distance of two kilometers by 48.0 per cent. Thus, private health

Table 4.4.1A: Communication and Education.

	Distance	Caste				Total
		Madiga	Mala	Adavi Golla	Boya	
1	2	3	4	5	6	7
Bus Stand	within the village	53 (84.1)	6 (100.0)	31 (31.0)	40 (66.7)	130 (56.8)
	< 2	0 (0.0)	0 (0.0)	48 (48.0)	20 (33.3)	68 (29.7)
	3-5	10 (15.9)	0 (0.0)	11 11.0)	0 .0)	21 9.2)
	NA	0 .0)	0 (0.0)	10 (10.0)	0 (0.0)	10 (4.4)
	Total	63 (100.0)	6 (100.0)	100 (100.0)	60 (100.0)	229 (100.0)
Primary School	within the village	52 (82.5)	6 (100.0)	90 (90.0)	50 (83.3)	198 (86.5)
	< 2	11 (17.5)	0 (0.0)	10 (10.0)	10 (16.7)	31 (13.5)
	Total	63 (100.0)	6 (100.0)	100 (100.0)	60 (100.0)	229 (100.0)

1	2	3	4	5	6	7
High School	within the village	29 (46.0)	1 (16.7)	11 (11.0)	20 (33.3)	61 (26.6)
	< 2	14 (22.2)	5 (83.3)	60 (60.0)	40 (66.7)	119 (52.0)
	3 – 5	10 (15.9)	0 (0.0)	29 (29.0)	0 (0.0)	39 (17.0)
	6 >	10 (15.9)	0 (0.0)	0 (0.0)	0 (0.0)	10 (4.4)
	Total	63 (100.0)	6 (100.0)	100 (100.0)	60 (100.0)	229 (100.0)

1	2	3	4	5	6	7
	6 >	29 (46.0)	0 (0.0)	40 (40.0)	10 (16.7)	79 (34.5)
	Total	63 (100.0)	6 (100.0)	100 (100.0)	60 (100.0)	229 (100.0)
Anganwadi	within the village	59 (93.7)	1 (16.7)	100 (100.0)	60 (100.0)	220 (96.1)
	< 2	4 (6.3)	5 (83.3)	0 (0.0)	0 (0.0)	9 (3.9)
	Total	63 (100.0)	6 (100.0)	100 (100.0)	60 (100.0)	229 (100.0)
Anganwadi Centre	within the village	63 (100.0)	6 (100.0)	100 (100.0)	60 (100.0)	229 (100.0)
	Total	63 (100.0)	6 (100.0)	100 (100.0)	60 (100.0)	229 (100.0)
Private Health Facility	within the village	43 (68.3)	6 (100.0)	10 (10.0)	20 (33.3)	79 (34.5)
	< 2	20 (31.7)	0 (0.0)	50 (50.0)	40 (66.7)	110 (48.0)

1	2	3	4	5	6	7
	3 – 5	0 (0.0)	0 (0.0)	20 (20.0)	0 (0.0)	20 (8.7)
	6 >	0 (0.0)	0 (0.0)	20 (20.0)	0 (0.0)	20 (8.7)
	Total	63 (100.0)	6 (100.0)	100 (100.0)	60 (100.0)	229 (100.0)

TABLE 4.4.1C: Health Professionals.

Health Professionals	Distance	Caste				Total
		Madiga	Mala	Adavi Golla	Boya	
1	2	3	4	5	6	7
ANM/Nurse	within the village	51 (81.0)	3 (50.0)	0 (0.0)	60 (100.0)	114 (49.8)
	< 2	2 (3.2)	3 (50.0)	50 (50.0)	0 (0.0)	55 24.0)
	3 – 5	10 15.9)	0 .0)	40 40.0)	0 (0.0)	50 (21.8)
	6 >	0 (0.0)	0 (0.0)	10 (10.0)	0 (0.0)	10 (4.4)
	Total	63 (100.0)	6 (100.0)	100 (100.0)	60 (100.0)	229 (100.0)
Health Worker	within the village	59 (93.7)	3 (50.0)	12 (12.0)	60 (100.0)	134 (58.5)
	< 2	4 (6.3)	3 (50.0)	38 (38.0)	0 (0.0)	45 (19.7)

1	2	3	4	5	6	7
	3 – 5	0 (0.0)	0 (0.0)	50 (50.0)	0 (0.0)	50 (21.8)
	Total	63 (100.0)	6 (100.0)	100 (100.0)	60 (100.0)	229 (100.0)
Doctor	within the village	14 (22.2)	6 (100.0)	0 (0.0)	23 (38.3)	43 (18.8)
	< 2	29 (46.0)	0 (0.0)	20 (20.0)	20 (33.3)	69 (30.1)
	3 – 5	10 (15.9)	0 (0.0)	40 (40.0)	3 (5.0)	53 (23.1)
	6 >	10 (15.9)	0 (0.0)	40 (40.0)	14 (23.3)	64 (27.9)
	Total	63 (100.0)	6 (100.0)	100 (100.0)	60 (100.0)	229 (100.0)

facility is more easily accessible to the majority. A large percentage of Adavi Golla members do not have access to both government and private health facilities.

The services Anganwadi and Anganwadi Workers are however, available either within the village or at a distance of within two kilometers for all the communities. Health sub-centre is also another health facility which is very proximate to the members under reference.

Our analysis reveals that the health services of health professional and medical facilities are accessible at a reasonable distance for majority of the respondents and communities under reference. The only exception however is Adavi Golla members. The gratifying feature is that a prepondering majority of Scheduled Caste members under reference have access to these facilities either within village or within a distance of two kilometers.

ACCESS TO DRINKING WATER AND FOOD

Safe potable drinking water is a must for good health. The primary cause for morbidity and disease is due to polluted drinking water. Anantapur District being a drought area, water is scarce commodity. Yet our data shows that majority of respondents (64.2 per cent) are provided with drinking water by public tap system. 5.7 per cent of respondents have their own tap connections. 19.2 per cent however depend upon tank water for drinking purposes. 10.9 per cent depend upon bore wells. Only Adavi Golla members depend upon tank water (44.0 per cent). Around 17 per cent of Madiga and Boya members under reference depend on bore wells.

Government of Andhra Pradesh provides ration (rice) at highly subsidized price to the poor. For this purpose the poor are identified and are provided with white colour ration card. Each card-holder is eligible to get 20 kgs. of rice per month. This provision guarantees the minimum subsistence. More often however, this gesture reduces the burden of poverty and hunger. Our data shows that all 229 respondents under reference have been provided with the white colour ration card.

REFERENCES

Ananda Row, T. 1901. 'Census of India 1901', Vol. XXIV. Government Printing Press, Bangalore.

Ananthakrishna Iyer, L.K. 1930. 'The Mysore Tribes and Castes', The Mysore Government Press, Bangalore, Vol. III, pp.197-217.

Berger, J. 2004. 'Re-sexualizing the epidemic: Desire, risk and HIV prevention', Development Update, 5 (3), 45-67, Johannesburg.

Green ME & Merrick T., 2005. 'Poverty reduction: Does reproductive health matter?', HNP discussion paper, World Bank, Washington DC.

Hassan, S.S. 1920. 'Castes and Tribes of the H.E.H. The Nizam's Dominions Hyderabad State', The Times Press, Bombay.

Hemminki E., Sihvo S., Koponen P. and Kosumen E. 'Quality of contraceptive services in Finland', Qual Health Care, 1997; 6:62-68.

Matthews Z., Ramakrishna J., Mahendra S., Kilaru A., Ganapathy S., 2005. 'Birth rights and rituals in rural South India: care seeking in the intrapartum period', Journal of Biosocial Science, 37 (4), 385-411.

Molesworth K., 2005. 'The impact of transport provision on direct and proximate determinants of access to health services', Swiss Tropical Institute.

Murphy EM, Greene ME, Mihailovic A., Olupot-Olupot P. 2006. 'Was the "ABC" approach (abstinence, being faithful, using condoms) responsible for Uganda's decline in HIV?', PLoS Med. 3 (9): e379. DOI: 10.1371/journal.pmed.0030379.

Nanjundayya, H.V. and Ananthakrishna Iyer, L.K. 1931. 'The Mysore Tribes and Castes, The Mysore University, Mysore, Vol. IV, pp.125-169.

Rami Reddy, V., Gunasundaramma, G.P. Naidu, B.K.C Reddy and K.R.S. Reddy, 1980. 'ABO and Rh(D) Blood Groups in Ten Population of Sri Venkateswara University Area, South India', Indian Journal of Heredity, 12 (3), pp. 71-119.

Singh, K.S. 1998. 'India's Communities', Oxford University Press, New Delhi, Vol. V.

Singh, K.S. 1998. 'India's Communities',Oxford University Press, New Delhi, Vol. IV.

Thruston, E., 1909. 'Castes and Tribes of Southern India' Madras: Government Press, Madras; rpt. 1975, Cosmo Publications, Delhi), Vol. II, pp. 284-295.

Thruston, E., 1909. 'Castes and Tribes of Southern India' Madras: Government Press, Madras; rpt. 1975; Cosmo Publications, Delhi), Vol. VI, pp. 292-325.

Thruston, E., Castes and Tribes of Southern India (Madras: Government Press, 1090; rpt. 1975, Delhi; Cosmo Publications), Vol. I.

CHAPTER 5

Reproductive Health: Analysis and Discussions of the Study

Specific reproductive events, notably pregnancy and child bearing have an impact on women's health as well as on traditionally emphasized demographic trends. The concept of Reproductive Health brings a new dimension to safe motherhood, family planning and STD programmes. Integrating them so that they are not delivered in isolation enables communities to deal in a more comprehensive manner in order to overcome the issue of territoriality.

Therefore, in the present Chapter, the analysis of the third, fourth and the fifth objectives of the study are presented. Thereby an attempt is made to present the reproductive health status and the practices. For this purpose, the present Chapter is divided into three Sections. The first section provides the analysis of reproductive health status; reproductive health practices are presented in the second section; and the third section provides the analysis of social exclusion and social inclusion of reproductive health care of the respondents under study.

SECTION I

REPRODUCTIVE HEALTH STATUS

Reproductive health status in this is examined with reference to current marital status, age; age at marriage; and childbearing.

Marriage in the household in India is an important event. Marriage in India marks the point in a woman's life when childbearing becomes socially acceptable. Marriage is thus, a principal indicator of women's exposure to the risk of pregnancy. Age at first marriage has a profound impact on childbearing and thus on reproductive health because women who marry early have on average have a longer period of exposure to pregnancy and a greater number of lifetime births. Therefore, early age at marriage in a population is usually associated with a longer period of exposure to the risk of pregnancy and higher fertility levels.

CURRENT MARITAL STATUS AND AGE

Current marital status refers to marital status at the time of the survey. All the respondents under study are currently married. Their current age ranges between 17 years to 56 years. The average age of the respondents under study is found to be 31.41 years. Caste-wise Mala women are older in their average age (32.50 years). Currently the youngest married person is 17 years old and the oldest is 55 years. Among Adavi Golla, Boya and Madiga caste women the youngest is found to be 17 yers, 19 years, 20 years and the oldest is 55 years, 40 years, 56 years respectively. The average age is found to be 31.69 years, 30.60 years and 31.62 years respectively. However, 27.51 per cent of respondents belong to the age group of 19 to 25 years. Only 1.30 per cent of women under reference are aged 18 years. A larger percentage (46.28) is aged more than 31 years.

A comparison of field data with national data reveals that current marital status is universal in the field area. Where as at national level, One-fifth of Indian women age 15-49 have never been married. Seventy-five per cent are currently married, less than 1 per cent are married but *gauna* has not been performed, 3 per cent are widowed, and 1 per cent are divorced, separated, or deserted (NFHS 3, 2007).

The proportion of women and men who are married young has important policy and programme implications. At the national level, 27 per cent of 15-19 year old women are currently married (15 per cent of urban women and 33 per cent of rural women) (NFHS 3, 2007).

However, in our study this proportion of young married women (15-19 years) is very less. Only 1.30 per cent of women under reference are aged 18 years. 27.51 per cent of respondents belong to the age group of 19 to 25 years. A larger percentage (46.28) is aged more than 31 years.

AGE AT MARRIAGE

Our data reveals that the average age of the respondents at their first marriage is 18.21 years. However, 40.17 per cent were found to be married below 17 years age at marriage. 2.6 per cent of the respondents were married at 14 years and below years of age. 6.1 per cent and 17.0 per cent were married at the age of 15 years and 16 years respectively.

A sizable percentage (24.5 per cent) was married between 19-25 years age. Another large percentage (33.2) was married at the age of 18 years. The DLHS (2002-04) Anantapur District data reveals that the mean age at marriage is 18.5 years and girls married below the legal at marriage is 38.8 per cent.

The respondents who were married at a very young age (10-14 years) are found to be 6.3 per cent and 2.0 per cent among Madiga and Adavi Golla Communities respectively. Similarly the women under reference who were married between 14-17 years age is found to be 41.25 per cent; 52.0 per cent and 14.4 per cent among Madiga, Adavi Golla, Boya Communities respectively. Our data points out those marriages below the legal age are more prevalent and common among Adavi Golla Community. Larger percentage of marriages 34.9 per cent, 21.0 per cent, 28.0 per cent among Madiga, Adavi Golla and Boya Communities respectively is however found to be at exact legal age of 18 years.

More than one-quarter (27 per cent) of Indian women age 20-49 married before age 15; over half (58 per cent) married before the legal minimum marriage age of 18, and three-quarters (74 per cent) married before reaching age 20 (NFHS 3, 2007).

The mean age at marriage among the boys and girls in the country as 24.5 and 19.5 years respectively. One-fifth of the boys and a little more than one-fourth of the girls in India got married before attaining the minimum legal age at marriage of 21 and 18 years respectively.

The comparison of field data with national and district level data reveals that the mean age at marriage for women under reference (18.21 years) is lower than the district average (18.5 years); and national mean age 19.5 years. The percentage of women age 15-49 married below the legal age at marriage of 18 years is found to be 40.1 per cent which is lesser than national average (58 per cent; NFHS-3, 2007); but higher than the district (38.8 per cent). However, only 27.27 per cent women 15-25 were found to be married below 18 years.

Table 5.1.1: Distribution of Respondents by Age at Marriage and Caste

Age at marriage	Caste				Total
	Madiga	Mala	Adavi Golla	Boya	
10-14	4 (6.3)	0 (0.0)	2 (2.0)	0 (0.0)	6 (2.6)
15	5 (7.9)	0 (0.0)	8 (8.0)	1 (1.7)	14 (6.1)
16	12 (19.0)	0 (0.0)	21 (21.0)	6 (10.0)	39 (17.0)
17	5 (7.9)	0 (0.0)	21 (21.0)	7 (11.7)	33 (14.4)
18	22 (34.9)	4 (66.7)	21 (21.0)	29 (48.3)	76 (33.2)
19-25	13 (20.6)	2 (33.3)	24 (24.0)	17 (28.3)	56 (24.5)
NA	2 (3.2)	0 (0.0)	3 (3.0)	0 (0.0)	5 (2.2)
Total	63 (100.0)	6 (100.0)	100 (100.0)	60 (100.0)	229 (100.0)
Mean age	17.58	19.33	18.01	18.76	18.21
Percentage of Marriage Below Legal Age	41.25	19.33	52.0	23.33	40.17

CHILD BEARING

Child bearing is an important event and also a process in the women's life. It also poses great threat to women's life and health. Not only is the risk of dying from maternal causes high, but also, women in India are repeatedly exposed to theses risks as a result of high and closely spaced fertility stretching from adolescence to menopause.

The life time risk of dying from pregnancy related causes in India-with a total fertility rate of 4-5 and a maternal mortality ratio of around 500 per 10,000 live births – is as high as one in 27 (Royston and Armstrong, 1989). Maternal deaths in India account for about one per cent of all deaths and two per cent of all female deaths annually-but this translates into over ten per cent of all deaths among women in the reproductive ages and 13.2 per cent among rural women in 1987 (UNICEF, 1991).

Table 5.1.2: Distribution of Respondents by Age at Marriage and Current Age.

Age at marriage	Current age				Total
	15-25	26-35	36-45	46 >	
1	2	3	4	5	6
	2	1	2	1	6
10-14	(33.3)	16.7)	(33.3)	(16.7)	100.0)
	(3.0)	1.0)	(4.4)	(7.7)	(2.6)
	(0.9)	(0.4)	(0.9)	(0.4)	(2.6)
	2	8	3	1	14
15	(14.3)	(57.1)	(21.4)	(7.1)	(100.0)
	(3.0)	(7.6)	(6.7)	(7.7)	(6.1)
	(0.9)	(3.5)	(1.3)	(0.4)	(6.1)
	7	17	11	4	39
16	(17.9)	(43.6)	(28.2)	(10.3)	(100.0)
	(10.6)	(16.2)	(24.4%)	(30.8)	(17.0)
	(3.1)	(7.4)	(4.8)	(1.7)	(17.0)
	7	18	6	2	33
17	(21.2)	(54.5)	(18.2)	(6.1)	(100.0)
	(10.6)	(17.1)	(13.3)	(15.4)	(14.4)
	(3.1)	(7.9)	(2.6)	(0.9)	(14.4)
	28	32	13	3	76
18	(36.8)	(42.1)	(17.1)	(3.9)	(100.0)
	(42.4)	(30.5)	(28.9)	(23.1)	(33.2)
	(12.2)	(14.0)	(5.7)	(1.3)	(33.2)

1	2	3	4	5	6
	19	27	9	1	56
19-25	(33.9)	(48.2)	(16.1)	(1.8)	(100.0)
	(28.8)	(25.7)	(20.0)	(7.7)	(24.5)
	(8.3)	(11.8)	(3.9)	(0.4)	(24.5)
	1	2	1	1	5
NA	(20.0)	(40.0)	(20.0)	(20.0)	(100.0)
	(1.5)	(1.9)	(2.2)	(7.7)	(2.2)
	(0.4)	(0.9)	(0.4)	(0.4)	(2.2)
	66	105	45	13	229
Total	(28.8)	(45.9)	(19.7)	(5.7)	(100.0)
	(100.0)	(100.0)	(100.0)	(100.0)	(100.0)
	(28.8)	(45.9)	(19.7)	(5.7)	(100.0)
Means age	18.63				18.21
Percentage of Married Below 18 Years (10-17)	27.27				40.17

There are very few community or household level studies of maternal mortality. Notable among these is a 1985-86 village level study in Anantapur, Andhra Pradesh, which found a ratio of 830 and 545 in rural and urban areas respectively (Bhatia, 1988). Maternal deaths accounted for 38 per cent of all deaths to women in the reproductive ages in rural areas and 28 per cent in urban. Maternal mortality ranges from 2166 per 100000 live births in the least developed villages (as measured by location, communication and transport facilities, educational land and other amenities), to 1523 and 803 respectively among somewhat and adequately developed villages, to 516 in highly developed villages. As many as 66 per cent of maternal deaths had not been recorded by health workers; reasons could range from inability in attributing cause of death to simply a vested interest in minimizing reported maternal deaths.

Unfortunately, maternal deaths are notoriously under-reported even in the more developed world, since often when the cause of death is a non-obstetric condition, precipitated by an obstetric condition, the latter is not reported; underestimates in the range of 33-50 per cent have thus been observed even in the USA (Royston and Armstrong, 1989).

Therefore, in the present study childbearing is examined with reference to age at first birth, and number of children ever born (fertility).

AGE AT FIRST BIRTH

The age at which women start childbearing is an important demographic determinant of fertility. A higher median age at first birth is an indicator of lower fertility. The early onset of childbearing has disturbing consequences for reproductive health. It is estimated that as many as 10-15 per cent of all births annually occur to women in their early teens, before they are physically fully developed (Mathai, 1989; Kapil, 1990).

The extra nutritional demands of pregnancy come at the heels of the adolescent growth spurt, which itself requires additional nutritional inputs, and results in the poor nutritional status of the pregnant adolescent (Ramachandran, 1989). As a result of combined effects of shorter average maternal height, competition for nutrients between the mother's growth needs and the growth needs of her foetus, and also due to poorer placental function of adolescent mothers, the risks of maternal mortality and peri-and neonatal mortality are exceptionally high among adolescents (Leslie, 1991).

Hence it is not surprising to note that maternal deaths are concentrated in the youngest ages; 1986 data from rural India suggest that as many as 45 per cent of all maternal deaths took place among women aged under 24 (Registrar General, 1987; rates for adolescents are not separately available).

Estimates derived from Bhatia's villages' level study in Andhra Pradesh (Acsadi and Johnson-Acsadi, 1990) suggest that adolescent maternal mortality ratios are almost twice as high as those reported for women ages 25-39 1484 per 10000 live births among women aged 15-19 compared to 735, 708 and 736 for women age 25-29, 3034, and 35-39 respectively.

Not only are adolescent mothers more likely to die or suffer from morbidity, but the children they bear are also exposed to considerable risk.

First birth at the age of 18 years and less is found to be 29.31 per cent among the women aged 15-25 years under reference. Our data reveals that 28.22 per cent of respondent's aged 15-49 have given birth to their first child before they attained 18 years of age. But majority (61.1 per cent) was in the age group of 19 to 25 years. 0.9 per cent each however, has given birth at the age of 14 years and 15 years respectively.

Caste-wise analysis of our data reveals the following trends. Adolescent (14 to 18 years) child births are more than 16 per cent among Adavi Golla (38.7 per cent), Boya (16.66 per cent) and Madiga (19.14) Communities. More specifically, among Adavi Gollas adolescent child births were 38.70 per cent; 16.7 per cent in Boya Community; and 19.14 per cent among Madiga Community.

According to NFHS-3 the median age at first birth for women among women age 20-49 years by current age according to caste for Scheduled Castes was 19.00 years and for other backward castes 19.6 years. Further the report reveals that five per cent of women age 25-49 have given birth by age 15. The percentage who gave births by age 15 decreases steadily from six per cent among women age 35-39 to one per cent among women aged 15-19. 30 per cent of women age 25-49 gave births before age 18 and 53 per cent gave births by age 20.

Table 5.1.3: Distribution of Respondents by Age at First Birth & Caste

Age* at First Birth	Caste				Total
	Madiga	Mala	Adavi Golla	Boya	
10-14	1 (1.6)	0 (0.0)	1 (1.0)	0 (0.0)	2 (0.9)
15	2 (3.2)	0 (0.0)	0 (0.0)	0 (0.0)	2 (0.9)
16	0 (0.0)	0 (0.0)	9 (9.0)	0 (0.0)	9 (3.9)
17	0 (0.0)	0 (0.0)	6 (6.0)	0 (0.0)	6 (2.6)
18	6 (9.5)	0 (0.0)	22 (22.0)	10 (16.7)	38 (16.6)
19-25	36 (57.1)	6 (100.0)	56 (56.0)	42 (70.0)	140 (61.1)
26-30	2 (3.2)	0 (0.0)	2 (2.0)	0 (0.0)	4 (1.7)
31>	0 (0.0)	0 (0.0)	0 (0.0)	1 (1.7)	1 (0.4)
NA	16 25.4)	0 (0.0)	4 (4.0)	7 (11.7)	27 (11.8)
Total	63 (100.0)	6 (100.0)	100 (100.0)	60 (100.0)	229 (100.0)
Mean at First Birth	21.28		20.25	21.45	20.85
Percentage of women who gave first birth below 18 and less years	19.14	Nil	38.00	16.66	28.22

Our data reveals that 0.5 per cent each of the women category aged 36 years and above and women aged 26 to 35 years gave birth at the age of 14 and 15 years respectively. 2.6 per cent of women and 2.7 per cent of women above the age of 26 years gave births at the 16 and 17 years respectively. 17.6 per cent of the women aged above 26 years under reference have given birth below the age of 18 years. This is far lesser than the national figures.

CHILDREN EVER BORN

Among women aged 15-49 in India who are currently married, the mean number of children ever born and living is 2.85. The mean number of children ever bore increases steadily with age, reaching a high of 4.24 children for currently married women aged 45-49. Early child bearing is fairly common in India. 44 per cent of currently married women aged 15-19 years have already had a child (NFHS-3, 2007). On the average women who are completing reproductive period have given birth to four children in their reproductive life of which 3.5 children are surviving on the average (DLHS-2002-04, 2006).

It is found that the mean number of children born among the women aged 15.25 years is 1.62. Our data reveals that the mean number of children ever born and living 2.26 for women aged between 15-49 years under reference. Caste-wise the mean number of children ever born is highest among Mala Community (3.17) followed by Adavi Golla (2.4); Madiga 2.06 and Boya 2.05.

In our study sample the second order births are 37.6 per cent. The third order birth constitutes 24.5 per cent. The fourth and above constitute only 12.7 per cent. The third and above order births are found to be less in age group 26-35 years (42.0 per cent) rather than 36-45 (68.8 per cent) and 46 years above years (53.9). Among the women aged 15-25 years, the third order plus births are found to be only 6.00 per cent.

Table 5.1.4: Age at First Birth and Current Age.

Age at First Birth	Current age				Total
	15-25	26-35	36-45	36 >	
1	2	3	4	5	6
10-14	1	0	0	1	2
	(50.0)	(0.0)	(0.0)	(50.0)	(100.0)
	(1.5)	(0.0)	(0.0)	(7.7)	(0.9)
	(0.4)	(0.0)	(0.0)	(0.4)	(0.9)
15	1	1	0	0	2
	(50.0)	(50.0)	(0.0)	(0.0)	(100.0)
	(1.5)	(1.0)	(0.0)	(0.0)	(0.9)
	(0.4)	(0.4)	(0.0)	(0.0)	(0.9)
16	3	5	1	0	9
	(33.3)	(55.6)	(11.1)	(0.0)	(100.0)
	(4.5)	(4.8)	(2.2)	(0.0)	(3.9)
	(1.3)	(2.2)	(0.4)	(0.0)	(3.9)
17	0	2	2	2	6
	(0.0)	(33.3)	33.3)	33.3)	100.0)
	(0.0)	(1.9)	(4.4)	(15.4)	(2.6)
	(0.0)	(0.9)	(0.9)	(0.9)	(2.6)
18	12	16	7	3	38
	(31.6)	(42.1)	(18.4)	(7.9)	(100.0)
	(18.2)	(15.2)	(15.6)	(23.1)	(16.6)
	(5.2)	(7.0)	(3.1)	(1.3)	(16.6)
19-25	41	69	26	4	140
	(29.3)	(49.3)	(18.6)	(2.9)	(100.0)
	(62.1)	(65.7)	(57.8)	(30.8)	(61.1)
	(17.9)	(30.1)	(11.4)	(1.7)	(61.1)
26-30	0	1	2	1	4
	(0.0)	(25.0)	(50.0)	(25.0)	(100.0)

1	2	3	4	5	6
	(0.0)	(1.0)	(4.4)	(7.7)	(1.7)
	(0.0)	(0.4)	(0.9)	(0.4)	(1.7)
	0	0	1	0	1
31>	(0.0)	(0.0)	(100.0)	(0.0)	(100.0)
	(0.0)	(0.0)	(2.2)	(0.0)	(0.4)
	(0.0)	(0.0)	(0.4)	(0.0)	(0.4)
	8	11	6	2	27
NA	(29.6)	(40.7)	(22.2)	(7.4)	(100.0)
	(12.1)	(10.5)	(13.3)	(15.4)	(11.8)
	(3.5)	(4.8)	(2.6)	(0.9)	(11.8)
	66	105	45	13	229
Total	(28.8)	(45.9)	(19.7)	(5.7)	(100.0)
	(100.0)	(100.0)	(100.0)	(100.0)	(100.0)
	(28.8)	(45.9)	(19.7)	(5.7)	(100.0)
Mean age	20.60				20.85
Percentage of women who give first birth below 18 and less years	29.31				28.22

Caste-wise the third order and above births are found to be more among Mala Community (83.33 per cent) followed by Adavi Golla Community (41.0 per cent); and 31 per cent each among Boya and Madiga Communities.

Thus our data pointes out that number of children ever born vary by age and by caste. The mean average number of children born and living is however, lesser than national average. Even caste wise the national average children ever born for women belonging to Scheduled Castes and Other Backward Classes is 2.9 and 2.7 respectively (DLHS-2002-04, 2006). Whereas in our study the average No. of children ever born to the women of Backward Classes is only 2.2 and for Scheduled Castes 2.6.

Similarly the occurrence of births of the third order and above is more among women from Scheduled Caste (46.0 per cent), Other Backward Class (42.0 per cent) at National Level. Whereas our study reversal that the births of third order and above are more among the Scheduled Castes (57.54 per cent) which is higher than the National Average; the same is however lower in case of Backward Classes (36.33 per cent) which lesser than National Average.

Table 5.1.5: Number of Living Children and Caste.

No. of Living Children	Caste				Total
	Madiga	Mala	Adavi Golla	Boya	
1	19 (30.2)	0 (0.0)	18 (18.0)	8 (13.3)	45 (19.7)
2	20 (31.7)	1 (16.7)	38 (38.0)	25 (41.7)	84 (36.7)
3	15 (23.8)	2 (33.3)	25 (25.0)	20 (33.3)	62 (27.1)
4	4 (6.3)	2 (33.3)	13 (13.0)	1 (1.7)	20 (8.7)
5	2 (3.2)	0 (0.0)	2 (2.0)	0 (0.0)	4 (1.7)
6	0 (0.0)	1 (16.7)	1 (1.0)	1 (1.7)	3 (1.3)
No Living Children	3 (4.8)	0 (0.0)	3 (3.0)	5 (8.3)	11 (4.8)
Total	63 (100.0)	6 (100.0)	100 (100.0)	60 (100.0)	229 (100.0)

SECTION II

REPRODUCTIVE HEALTH PRACTICES

In this Section the reproductive health practices of the respondents are examined with reference to birth delivery practices, maternal healthcare practices and knowledge about reproductive tract infections.

Table 5.1.6: Number of Living Children and Age

No. of Living Children	Age				Total
	15-25	26-35	36-45	46 >	
0	8 (12.1)	2 (1.9)	0 (0.0)	1 (7.7)	11 (4.8)
1	26 (39.4)	12 (11.4)	5 (11.1)	2 (15.4)	45 (19.7)
2	28 (42.4)	45 (42.9)	7 (15.6)	4 (30.8)	84 (36.7)
3	3 (4.5)	35 (33.3)	22 (48.9)	2 (15.4)	62 (27.1)
4	1 (1.5)	9 (8.6)	8 (17.8)	2 (15.4)	20 (8.7)
5	0 (0.0)	1 (1.0)	2 (4.4)	1 (7.7)	4 (1.7)
6	0 (0.0)	1 (1.0)	1 (2.2)	1 (7.7)	3 (1.3)
Total	66 (100.0)	105 (100.0)	45 (100.0)	13 (100.0)	229 (100.0)

Birth Delivery practices assumes importance in the context of high rate of maternal mortality in India. The place of birth delivery and the professional assistance for the conduct of safe delivery are two important factors/ practices at the time of birth delivery which have a bearing on maternal mortality.

PLACE OF DELIVERY

In India traditionally, birth deliveries are conducted at home, and are generally assisted by a traditional midwife (Manthrasani) or by the elderly women to cut the umbilical cord. The delivery practices and the method of cutting the umbilical cord are crude and unhygienic and often result in high rates of mortality- both maternal as well as infant mortality. Therefore, analysis of the place of birth delivery and assistance at delivery assumes importance.

The analysis of birth delivery practices reveals interesting trends. Our analysis reveals a progressive decline in the birth deliveries at home. It is found 41.5 per cent of first deliveries occurred at home. The deliveries at home have declined to 24 per cent by third birth delivery.

While the importance of institutional birth deliveries is gaining greater acceptance, the credibility and acceptance of government run maternity institutions are losing faith and credibility. Our data shows that 42.8 per cent of the first deliveries were at government institutions like P.H.C., Government Hospital. But this has declined to 7.4 per cent by third birth delivery. On the other hand only 4.8 per cent deliveries were at private health facility during the first delivery; which has increased to 24.9 per cent by third delivery. The primary health centres were least preferred centres for birth deliveries.

Institutional deliveries, particularly birth delivery at private health facility are being increasingly favoured by the Scheduled Castes. Cent per cent and 68.3 per cent of third birth deliveries among Mala and Madiga Communities respectively were at private health facility. None of the birth deliveries were at primary health centres. Birth deliveries at Government Hospital have declined from 49.2 per cent to 6.3 per cent among Madiga Community. Similar trend is observed in the case of Backward Classes too.

Our data further reveals that birth deliveries at home among Madiga community has declined from 39.7 per cent of first birth deliveries to 20.6 per cent of third birth deliveries. But birth deliveries at home continue to occur

Table 5.2.1: Caste & Place of Delivery by Number of Pregnancies.

Place of Delivery		Madiga			Mala			Adavi Golla			Boya			Total		
		1	2	3	1	2	3	1	2	3	1	2	3	1	2	3
Home	N	25	19	13	3	—	—	42	30	18	25	25	24	95	74	55
	%	39.7	30.2	20.6	50.	—	—	42.0	30.0	18.0	41.7	41.7	40.0	41.5	32.3	24.0
FHC	N	—	—	—	—	—	—	13	4	1	8	1	—	21	5	1
	%	—	—	—	—	—	—	13.0	4.0	1.0	13.3	1.7	—	9.2	2.2	0.4
Govt.	N	31	10	4	3	—	—	27	19	6	16	10	6	77	39	16
Hospital	%	49.2	15.9	6.3	50.0	—	—	27.0	19.0	6.0	26.7	16.7	10.0	33.6	17.0	7.0
Private	N	4	31	43	—	6	6	6	1	1	1	10	7	11	48	57
Hospital	%	6.3	49.2	68.3	—	100.0	100.0	6.0	1.0	1.0	1.7	16.7	11.7	4.8	21.0	24.9
No	N	3	3	3	—	—	—	12	46	74	10	14	23	25	63	100
Response	%	4.8	4.8	4.8	—	—	—	12.0	46.0	74.0	16.7	23.3	38.3	10.9	27.5	43.7
Total	N	63	63	63	6	6	6	100	100	100	60	60	60	229	229	229
	%	100.0	100.0	100.0	100.0	100.0	100.0	100.0	100.0	100.0	100.0	100.0	100.0	100.0	100.0	100.0

Note: 1 = First Pregnancy; 2 = Second Pregnancy; 3 = Third Pregnancy.

Table 5.2.2: Age & Place of Delivery by Number of Pregnancies.

Place of Delivery		15-25			26-35			36-45			46 >			Total		
		1	2	3	1	2	3	1	2	3	1	2	3	1	2	3
Home	N	17	16	12	45	33	26	23	19	15	10	6	2	95	74	55
	%	25.8	24.2	18.2	42.9	31.4	24.8	51.1	42.2	33.3	76.9	46.2	15.4	41.5	32.3	24.0
PHC	N	5	1	0	10	4	1	6	0	0	0	0	0	21	5	1
	%	7.6	1.5		9.5	3.8	1.0	13.3						9.2	2.2	0.4
Govt.	N	27	6	1	34	24	10	14	7	3	2	2	2	77	39	16
Hospital	%	40.9	9.1	1.5	32.4	22.9	9.5	31.1	15.6	6.7	15.4	15.4	15.4	33.6	17.0	7.0
Private	N	4	17	20	6	21	26	1	8	8	0	2	3	11	48	57
Hospital	%	6.1	25.8	30.3	5.7	20.0	24.8	2.2	17.8	17.8		15.4	23.1	4.8	21.0	24.9
No	N	13	26	33	10	23	42	1	11	19	1	3	6	25	63	100
Response	%	19.7	39.4	50.0	9.5	21.9	40.0	2.2	24.4	42.2	7.7	23.1	46.2	10.9	27.5	43.7
Total	N	66	66	66	105	105	105	45	45	45	13	13	13	229	229	229
	%	100.0	100.0	100.0	100.0	100.0	100.0	100.0	100.0	100.0	100.0	100.0	100.0	100.0	100.0	100.0

Note: 1 = First Pregnancy; 2 = Second Pregnancy; 3 = Third Pregnancy.

more in the case of Backward Classes particularly among Boya Community (40 per cent and above. In the case of Adavi Golla Community birth deliveries at home have declined from first birth delivery (42.0 per cent) to third birth delivery (18.0 per cent).

PROFESSIONAL ASSISTANCE AT THE TIME OF DELIVERY

The analysis of professional assistance at the time of birth delivery reveals encouraging trends. Unlike in the past that dependent on traditional mid-wife (Mantrasani) and on elderly women for birth delivery has greatly declined. Our data shows that 60.3 per cent of birth deliveries were assisted by trained health professionals like allopathic doctors (19.7 per cent) and ANM/Nurse (40.6 per cent). Very few birth deliveries were conducted by the traditional mid-wife (1.7 per cent) and elderly women (6.6 per cent). ANM/ Nurse is found to be more accessible to the members of all communities at the time of birth deliveries. It is pertinent mention here the services of health worker and ANM/ Nurse are available within village for 58.5 per cent and 49.8 per cent of the respondents respectively. The availability of doctor within the village is only for 18.8 per cent. Hence, the greater dependence on ANM/Nurse.

The services of ANM/Nurse are availed by more by Mala (66.7 per cent), Madiga (58.7 per cent) and Boya. The services of traditional mid-wife are availed by Madiga members (4.8 per cent). The services of elderly women are availed by Boya (11.7 per cent) and Madiga (9.5 per cent). The Adavi Gollas are at a disadvantage in terms of access to health facilities and as well as services of health professionals (see 4.4.1B and C).

TABLE 5.2.3: Delivery Assistant by Caste.

Assisted by	Madiga	Mala	Adavi Golla	Boya	Total
Doctor	9 (14.3)	0 (0.0)	24 (24.0)	12 (20.0)	45 (19.7)
ANM/Nurse	37 (58.7)	4 (66.7)	24 (24.0)	28 (46.7)	93 (40.6)
Dai/TBA/HW	3 (4.8)	2 (33.3)	15 (15.0)	0 (0.0)	20 (8.7)
Manthrasani	3 (4.8)	0 (0.0)	1 (1.0)	0 (0.0)	4 (1.7)
Elderly Women	6 (9.5)	0 (0.0)	2 (2.0)	7 (11.7)	15 (6.6)
Not Specified	5 (7.9)	0 (0.0)	34 (34.0)	13 (21.7)	52 (22.7)
Total	63 (100.0)	6 (100.0)	100 (100.0)	60 (100.0)	229 (100.0)

MATERNAL HEALTH CARE

The Maternal Health Care is provided through Antenatal Care Services. The present analysis is made with reference to supplementation of Iron Folic Acid Tablets (IFA) for reduction of Anemia, Tetanus Toxide Injection for immunization of expectant mothers, Full ANC Coverage of expectant mothers and visits by expectant mothers for ANC services.

SUPPLEMENTATION OF IFA

Our analysis reveals that a majority of expectant mothers are keen in receiving IFA supplementation. However, it observed that this keenness diminished progressively by pregnancy order and age.

Our data shows that 72.9 per cent of the respondents received full supplementation of IFA during their first pregnancy. During second pregnancy 50.2 per cent of respondents have accepted IFA supplementation. The acceptance of IFA supplementation has declined further during the third pregnancy and only 33.6 per cent have accepted IFA.

However, differential acceptance levels by caste are noticed for IFA supplementation. It observed that more than 80.0 per cent of the scheduled caste under reference and Boys have accepted IFA supplementation during first pregnancy. Only 56.0 per cent of Adavi Gollas have received IFA supplementation. During second pregnancy however more than 40.0 per cent in every caste under reference have accepted IFA. During third pregnancy however, only 25.4 per cent of Madiga have accepted IFA. Among backward classes the acceptance level is more than 30.0 per cent. Malas, however, were consistence in other three pregnancies and sent pre cent of them have received IFA.

Age-wise data shows that the acceptance of IFA is highest in the younger age group (15-25 years) which has progressively declined as the age group increases during first pregnancy. However, interestingly during the second pregnancy the acceptance of IFA was consistently more than 40.0 per cent for women between 15-45 of age group.

IMMUNIZATION

Our analysis shows that the acceptance of immunization has progressively decreased by pregnancy order. 31.4 per cent of the respondents had the required two and more number of injections. However, it is observed that the percentage of respondents is as high as 73.8 per cent if it is two and less number of TT injections during the first pregnancy. During the pregnancy this trend however, dropped down to 17.0 per cent in the case two and more

Table 5.2.4: Percentages of Maternal Care by Caste and Age

	Pregnancy		Caste					Age				
			Madiga	Mala	Adavi Golla	Boya	Total	15-25	26-35	36-45	46>	Total
1	2		3	4	5	6	7	8	9	10	11	12
IFA	I		85.7	100.0	56.0	85.0	**72.9**	84.8	74.3	62.2	38.5	**72.9**
	II		46.0	100.0	44.0	60.0	**20.2**	47.0	59.0	40.0	30.8	**20.2**
	III		25.4	100.0	34.0	35.0	**33.6**	27.3	35.2	40.0	30.8	**33.6**
TT	I		12.7	83.3	17.0	15.0	**17.0**	37.9	34.3	17.8	23.1	**17.0**
	II		19.0	83.3	24.0	23.0	**24.0**	25.8	27.6	13.3	23.1	**24.0**
	III		27.0	83.3	32.0	30.0	**31.4**	13.6	20.0	13.3	23.1	**31.4**
Full ANC	I		32.11	83.3	42.0	50.0	**48.0**	57.6	46.7	44.4	23.1	**48.0**
	II		54.0	83.3	38.0	41.7	**44.5**	50.0	46.7	37.8	23.1	**44.5**
	III		42.9	83.3	28.0	30.0	**34.1**	37.9	33.3	33.3	23.1	**34.1**
ANC-Checkups	I	1	57.1	83.3	47.0	88.3	**61.6**	69.7	63.8	55.6	23.1	**61.6**
		2	57.1	83.3	47.0	88.3	**61.6**	68.2	63.8	55.6	30.8	**61.6**
		3	49.2	66.7	41.0	86.7	**59.9**	59.1	59.0	51.1	30.8	**59.9**

1	2		3	4	5	6	7	8	9	10	11	12
	II	1	36.5	83.3	35.0	65.0	**44.5**	37.9	53.3	40.0	23.1	**44.5**
		2	39.7	83.3	34.0	58.3	**43.2**	36.4	52.4	35.6	30.8	**43.2**
		3	34.9	66.7	32.0	60.0	**41.0**	36.4	47.6	35.6	30.8	**41.0**
	III	1	22.2	83.3	27.0	38.3	**30.1**	19.7	34.3	37.8	23.1	**30.1**
		2	23.8	83.3	28.0	35.0	**30.1**	18.2	35.2	35.6	30.8	**30.1**
		3	22.2	66.7	27.0	33.0	**28.4**	18.2	32.4	33.3	30.8	**28.4**

Note: I = First Pregnancy. 1 = First Trimester.
II = Second Pregnancy. 2 = Second Trimester.
III = Third Pregnancy. 3 = Third Trimester.

TT injections and 32.8 per cent in the case of two and less number of TT injections.

Madigas and Boyas have shown least interest in receiving Tetanus Toxide immunization. Only 27.0 per cent of Madigas and 30.0 per cent of Boyas have received immunization during first pregnancy. During the third pregnancy only 12.7 per cent of Madiga and 15.0 per cent of Boyas have sought for immunization.

Age-wise, expectant mothers of 15-25 years have sought Tetanus Toxide immunization in larger percentages and this trend has declined as age and pregnancy order progressed. During the first pregnancy the women under 25 years age who sought immunization was 84.8 per cent (two and less number of TT injections) and 37.9 per cent (more than two TT injections).

FULL ANC

The analysis of full ANC coverage of the expectant mothers during their three pregnancies reveals that the mothers of all castes and of younger age group under reference were keen during their first pregnancy (48.0 per cent). The keenness of receiving full ANC coverage is diminished by pregnancy order.

Adavi Gollas are found to be less interested in receiving full ANC coverage than other communities under references. More than 30.0 per cent of the women age 15-45 have received full ANC even during their pregnancy.

The analysis of visits during three trimesters reveals that Boyas are consistent in all the three trimesters followed by Malas which is more than 80 per cent and 60.0 per cent during first and second pregnancies respectively. Adavi Gollas are found to be less keen in this regard.

It also observed that visits for ANC coverage were more consistent for the women aged 26-45 years in all three pregnancies and it was in consistent in the case of women aged 15-25 and 46 above years. Further it is observed lower percentage of frequencies during the third trimester period in all pregnancies.

PLACE OF ANC

Our data shows that a good percentage (31.0 per cent) received their ANC at Government Hospitals. Only 6.5 per cent have sought ANC from private health facility. 21.4 per cent received ANC from either PHC or its sub-centre. 11.8 per cent received ANC at their respective homes. 19.0 per cent of Adavi Gollas have received ANC at their home.

Table 5.2.5: Source of ANC and Caste

Source of ANC	Caste				Total
	Madiga	Mala	Adavi Golla	Boya	
ANM/Nurse	9 (14.3)	1 (16.7)	62 (62.0)	29 (48.3)	101 (44.1)
Govt. Doctor	3 (4.8)	4 (66.7)	9 (9.0)	4 (6.7)	20 (8.7)
Private Practicener	0 (0.0)	0 (0.0)	8 (8.0)	0 (0.0)	8 (3.5)
Any Others	1 (1.6)	0 (0.0)	0 (0.0)	0 (0.0)	1 (0.4)
Not Specified	50 (79.4)	1 (16.7)	21 (21.0)	27 (45.0)	99 (43.2)
Total	63 (100.0)	6 (100.0)	100 (100.0)	60 (100.0)	229 (100.0)

The source of ANC reveals that Adavi Gollas (62.0 per cent), Boyas (48.3 per cent) have received ANC through

ANM/Nurse. 79.4 per cent of Madiga community members have not specified the source of ANC. This implies the probability of discrimination/social exclusion on part of the paramedics. The analysis shows that ANM/Nurse play a vital role in extending ANC services to the weaker and marginalized sections.

Our analysis of seeking maternal health care in the form of antenatal care services reveals that the women under reference of all castes are encouraged to receive these services, particularly the women of younger age group. The analysis also reveals that Adavi Gollas among Backward Classes are still averse in seeking ANC services. The data shows the proximity of source of place of ANC services has greater impact on ANC coverage.

REPRODUCTIVE TRACK INFECTIONS (RTI)

Our fourth objective is to obtain data on the indicators of reproductive health with reference to reproductive track infections. This objective is perceived by examining status of education, problem of menstruation, experience of abnormal vaginal discharges and awareness of the symptoms of reproductive track infections.

STATUS AND PROBLEMS OF MENSTRUATION

Our data reveals that of the 229 respondents 55.0 per cent are currently menstruating; 2.6 per cent of pregnant, 29.3 per cent have reached the menopause stage. Thus, it is found more than 55.0 per cent are reproductively active. Our data further reveals during three months preceding the data collection, 40 respondents (17.5 per cent) reported that they have been experiencing problems with regard to menstruation.

An examination of the problems of menstruation reveals the following problems; irregular periods (3.1 per cent);

pain periods (4.4 per cent); frequent/short periods (1.3 per cent); delayed periods (1.7 per cent); prolonged bleeding (1.3 per cent). 1.7 per cent of the respondents experienced two of the above complaints; and 3.9 per cent experienced more than two such complaints. However, only 14 respondents from among the above 40 respondents have reported that duration of experience and medical consultation.

The duration of experience of above problems ranged from 12 months to 60 months period. Our data shows that 0.9 per cent of respondents have experiencing the problem for a period of 12 months; and another small percentage of respondents (0.4 per cent) for a period of 24 months. 3.9 per cent of respondents however, have been experiencing menstruation problems from more than 36 months period. Out of these 14 members who have longer duration of problem experience 9 members consulted government doctor; three members consulted private doctor; and one per cent did not seeking any medical care.

Above analysis reveals that women under reference feel either shy, insecure or complacent with regard to these gynecological problems and hesitate to seek medical consultation and care.

AWARENESS OF RTI SYMPTOMS

Experience of abnormal vaginal discharges its colour; odder, texture and duration is one of the indicators of reproductive health. It is found that nine women (3.9 per cent) under reference are experiencing abnormal vaginal discharges. Of these 9 persons five person's discharge stains the cloth; three person's discharge wets the cloths. Similarly eight persons discharge was white in colour and blood stain in one case; one discharge smell with foul odour. The experience of the symptom of abnormal discharge ranges between 24 months to 84 months. 8 members have been experiencing for more than 36 years. The symptoms are indicative uterine cervical cancer.

The following symptoms are indicative of reproductive track infections. Itching over vulva, warts/boils/ulcer around vulva, pain in lower abdominal not related to menses, pain during sexual intercourse, painful passage of urine and a combination of the above. It is found that 14 members (5.9 per cent) are only aware of these symptoms. Four members each have reported pain and lower abdomen not related to menses and bleeding during/after sexual intercourse. One per cent each has reported itching over vulva boils around vulva, pain during sexual intercourse and painful passage of urine. Two per have reported more than two combinations.

Thus our analysis of awareness of indicator of reproduction track infections reveals that a prepondering majority (85.0 and above per cent) are not aware of the indicators. The data also shows that a small percentage (5.9) have serious signs of reproductive tract infections. But this percentage in reality can be much more higher if a medical camp is organized.

SECTION III

REPRODUCTIVE HEALTH: SOCIAL EXCLUSION AND SOCIAL INCLUSION

The concept of Reproductive Health brings a new dimension to safe motherhood, family planning and STD programmes. Integrating them so that they are not delivered in isolation enables communities to deal in a more comprehensive manner in order to overcome the issue of territoriality.

Reproductive Health means more than bio-medical interventions. Reproductive Health affects, and is affected by, the broader context of people's lives – their economic circumstances, education, employment, living conditions, family environment, social and gender relationship, and the traditional and legal structures within which they live. It involves a greater awareness of health by individuals so that they can promote and protect their own reproductive health.

In this context, Population Health Research has taught us that social and health inequality hurts everyone, not just those at the bottom. Similarly, everyone is hurt by social exclusion - the groups and individuals who are marginalized and everyone collectively through the resulting deterioration in social cohesion. People's experience of exclusion can also be seen through the complex interaction of the social determinants. Each linkage between the determinants deepens a person's negative experience of exclusion, and over an individual's entire life cycle, the depth of exclusion is reinforced (Health Canada, 2001). Therefore, the key association between social inclusion and the social determinants is social and health inequities. Research also shows that the causal direction from social inequities to social exclusion to health inequities is multi-directional and mutually reinforcing in feedback loops (World Health Organization, 2005).

Decades of research have further shown that social exclusion impacts health and is aggravated by health status (World Health Organization, 2005). Social exclusion and a lack of participation in decision-making arising from deficits in the social determinants of health (SDOH) are major contributors to premature morbidity and death from chronic diseases, such as heart disease, stroke and diabetes (Wilkinson and Marmot, 1998).

Aspects of social exclusion are present in every domain of modern living including systems of education, employment, community life and citizenship. This broadness implies that the state should uphold standards of access

empower health status of its populace. Over the years it has adopted a two faced strategy to usher social inclusion. On one hand it strived to achieve overall socio-economic development with equity to influence and enhance the health status; and on the other it has attempted to raise the health status independent of socio-economic development through State intervention by extending health care with equity.

In view of the above reflections an attempt is made in this section to study **the practices of social exclusion and achievements of social inclusion** of reproductive health practices of a backward, indigenous and traditional communities in a chronically drought prone and backward district. For the purpose of analysis of social exclusion and social inclusion, broad parameters/indicators of reproductive health such as age at marriage, age at first birth, three plus order of births, immunization of expectant mothers, reduction of anemia, antenatal checkup, birth delivery practices access to health facilities and services are considered.

REPRODUCTIVE HEALTH STATUS: TRENDS OF SOCIAL EXCLUSION AND SOCIAL INCLUSION

Reproductive health addresses the reproductive processes, functions and systems at all stages of life. A reproductive health approach links demographic concerns, including fertility reduction with a range of objectives for improving the health and socio-economic status of women. It also proposes to address the needs of special target groups such as adolescents.

Socio-cultural factors which impinge reproductive health include **adolescent marriage**, strong seclusion norms which inhibit health-seeking, norms which encourage frequent and closely spaced pregnancies, and a general devaluation of women which makes them the last to obtain health care and which requires of them long periods of physical activity, large family size and women's lack of awareness of health practices.

Following marriage, there are socio-cultural pressures on the young women to conceive as soon as possible. This is one means whereby she can attain both prestige and security in her new home. Hence, adolescent marriage is synonymous with adolescent child bearing. Reproductive health exemplifies the complex interaction between biologic and gender differences. In some cases, these differences are manifested as social discrimination and lack of power to decide on one's reproductive health status. Oftentimes, the decision on what reproductive health status woman want, depends on their sexual partner, cultural orientation and oftentimes their health care provider. (Noel L. Espallardo, 2004).

Youth reproductive and sexual health has become a priority for policy-makers, programmers and researchers in India due to the country's large adolescent population and its high rates of child marriage and early childbearing. India has one of the highest rates of child marriage in the world, a practice that often results in early childbearing and thus serious reproductive health problems. The sluggish pace of increase in age at marriage is an important underlying factor for the poor reproductive health situation in the country.

The early onset of childbearing has disturbing consequences for reproductive health. A common consequence of early marriage and childbearing is that girls enter marriage and become mothers without adequate information about reproductive and sexual heath issues, including sexual intercourse, contraception, sexually transmitted infections (STIs), pregnancy and childbirth (Mensch et al. 1998; Singh and Samara, 1998). It is estimated that as many as 10-15 per cent of all births annually occur to women in their teens, before they are physically fully developed (Mathai, 1989; Kapil, 1990).

Because of social problems among adolescents, teenage pregnancy is an increasing problem in women's reproductive health. Teenage mothers and their children face poorer prospects in life than do women who delay motherhood until later in life. Early sexual intercourse, poor educational attainment, family background and interpersonal communication at home appear to be important factors that lead to increase probability of early pregnancy (Wellings, 1999).

The data relating to reproductive health status is presented in the Table 5.3.1. The data explains the reproductive health status with such indicators as: the mean age of women at marriage and the percentage of women marrying below the legal age of marriage; mean age at first birth; and the percentage of women having three plus children. And compares the same with district, state and national averages so as to assess the extent of social exclusion and social inclusion.

Analysis of our data shows that the mean age at marriage of the respondents under reference is 17.66 years. This is lower than national (19.5 years), state (18.4 years) and district (18.5 years) level mean age. In other words, early marriages akin to adolescent marriages still persists among Scheduled Caste and Backward Class. However, if examine age at marriage by current age there is considerable solace. The women of age 15-25 years are found to be married at mean age of 18.3 years which is an acceptable legal age at marriage. The lower mean age is due to the composition of higher age groups among the respondents. The data reveals that the respondents who's current age 25-49 years were married at mean age of 17.59 years.

These trends show that in recent years considerable effort have been made to raise the age at marriage and these efforts are paying results. Thus, the deprivation/ social exclusion of being married at a tender age is greatly reduced. This trend is further evident from the percentage of women marrying below the legal age.

Our data reveals that among the respondents aged 15-25 years; only 27.27 per cent were married below the legal age. On the contrary, among the women of the age 25-49, 32.31 per cent were married below the legal age. But the point however, is that the percentage of marriages below the legal age are higher than national level (28.0 per cent). Adolescent marriages are found to be in larger percentages among Madiga Community (41.1 per cent); Adavi Golla Community (52.0 per cent). Both these communities have deep connection with agrarian rural social structure and practice archaic practices.

Notwithstanding the early age at marriage the mean age at first birth among respondents is found to be 18.39 years this trend is consistent among the age group and caste groups under reference, with the exception of Madiga Community. Among Madiga members however, the mean age at first birth is found to be 15.87 years.

Percentage of women having three plus children is found to be higher among the respondents (38.8 per cent) which is higher than the district (21.7 per cent) and state (22.5 per cent) percentages but lower than national percentage (42.0 per cent). The percentage of women having three plus children is very small in the case of women aged 15-25 years (6.06 per cent) but understandably higher among the women aged 25-49 years (52.15 per cent).

Our analysis of reproductive health status reveals the following trends of social exclusion:

- Social exclusion persists with regard to age at first birth and marriage below the legal age at marriage. This trend is found to be in higher proportions in case of Madiga members (Scheduled Caste) and Adavi Golla Members (Backward Class).
- The social inclusion trends reveal that the district administration and health authorities efforts and the strategy of imparting better health status independent of socio-economic and cultural status is rewarding enough. Our data shows that there is appreciable rise in the age at marriage and age at first birth and great reduction in **3⁺ births** particularly among the young women aged 15-25 years and among castes which do not have greater involvement in the agrarian/rural occupation structure.

MATERNAL HEALTH CARE PRACTICES

Conduct of safe birth deliveries, immunization from Tetanus and reduction of anemia among expectant mothers; and monitoring and identifying risk factors during the pregnancy are the indicators of social exclusion and inclusion for maternal health care.

Traditionally women in rural India give birth at home. Inaccessibility of health facility and professional health services and poverty are the major causes for birth delivery at home. Thus, these birth deliveries are conducted under unhygienic conditions, without support of professional assistant and by crude practices often resulting in total consequences.

A birth delivery assisted by professional heath personnel like doctor/ANM/Nurse/Trained Birth Attendant either at home or institution is considered as safe delivery. Government of India is trying to achieve sent per cent institutional deliveries as one of its goal of reproductive heath.

Our data shows a large percentage (44.89 per cent) of birth deliveries among respondents were deliveries at home. This percentage though lower than the district (48.7 per cent) and national level (69.8 per cent), is higher than state level (38.6 per cent). Birth deliveries at home were found to be lower among women aged 15-25 (35.7 per cent) than the women aged 25-45 years (46.8 per cent).

Sixty nine per cent of the total deliveries among respondents were found to be safe deliveries, which are birth delivery assisted by health professionals. However, only 55.11 per cent of birth deliveries found to be institutional deliveries; and such deliveries are found to be more common among the women aged 15-25 years (64.29 per cent) than the women of higher age group (53.19 per cent). The percentage of institutional deliveries were however, found to be lower than the state level (60.9 per cent). The percentage of dependence on government institutions (31.86 per cent) for birth delivery is found to be higher than the private institutions (23.25).

But in the case of younger age group the birth deliveries were distributed more or less equally between government and private institutions. Intuitional deliveries are found to be in higher percentages for Scheduled Castes as more than 68 per cent of deliveries were institutional deliveries; whereas among Backward Classes it was found to around only 45.0 per cent.

Our analysis thus reveals that the Backward Castes are at a disadvantage and experience social exclusion as far as birth delivery practices are concerned. On the other hand greater equity is achieved in case of Scheduled Caste as cent per cent of deliveries among Mala Community and 77.8 per cent of deliveries among Madiga Community were safe deliveries.

IMMUNIZATION

Poor antenatal immunization results in neonatal tetanus. Tetanus is estimated to account for sum 230,000 to 280,000 infant deaths each year (Sokhey, 1998; Singh and Paul, 1988; UNICEF, 1991). Tetanus is held to account for anywhere between one-and-two thirds of all neonatal deaths (Kapil, 1980; Agarwar and Agarwal, 1987). The pregnant women are required to be immunized against tetanus by taking two or more tetanus toxide injections; or at least one tetanus toxide injection during their pregnancy.

Our data reveals the immunization of the pregnancy women is satisfactory. 75 per cent of the pregnant women have received at least one T.T. injection and another 17 per cent received more two T.T. injections. The immunization coverage is more than 90 per cent in caste groups. And particularly among the women aged 15-25 years. In other words as far as immunization concerned the social inclusion is highly satisfactory.

REDUCTION OF ANEMIA

Their exist in India a wide range of cultural practices regarding diet during pregnancy, both on how much and on what to eat. Unfortunately, these are unlikely to poster improvement in antenatal nutrition since they tend to discourage increases in women's already average daily food intake and in such nutritional items as leafy vegetables during pregnancy (Ramachandran, 1989). As a result, anemia is wide spread among pregnancy women (hemoglobin levels below 11 grams/dn); it is estimated to range from 50-70 per cent rural areas (UNICEF, 1991; Mathai, 1989), iron supplementation is found to improve such maternal health attributes such as weight gain, reduction in the incidence of anemia, complication during pregnancy (Iyengar,

1975; Dawn and Mitra, 1990). The national anaemia prophy laxis programme of iron an folic acid distribution was initiated as early as 1950s. In this programme pregnant women are provided with 100 iron and folic acid tables (IFA). The women who are pregnant are to be register in the first 12-16 weeks and must take IFA tables daily for hundred days (Ministry of Health and Family Welfare, 1997).

72.9 per cent of women have consumed adequate number of IFA tables during their pregnancy. This percentage is higher among the women aged 15-25 years (84.8 per cent). Caste-wise, the consumption of adequate IFA tablets is more than 85 per cent in all castes with exception of Adavi Gollas (56 per cent). Thus, our data shows the IFA supplementation coverage has successful and there is a greater social inclusion with regard to Scheduled Caste.

REDUCTION OF ANEMIA

Food and iron supplementation have been found to improve such maternal health attributes as weight gain, incidence of anaemia, complications during pregnancy and childbirth and birth weight (Dawn and Mitra, 1990; Iyengar, 1975).

As in the case of immunization the IFA supplementation to the pregnant mothers for reduction of anemia is found to be inconsistent. The supplementation of IFA tablets to the expected mothers of second pregnancy onwards is found to be poor. In other words the social exclusion is more with regard to the mothers with more pregnancies, higher age group and Madiga, Boya, Adavi Golla Communities. On the other hand greater social inclusion has been achieved in case of younger mothers particularly during their pregnancy.

ANTENATAL CARE SERVICE

It is observed that forty per cent of the expectant mothers were not covered by full ANC during their first pregnancy and this percentage increased in the subsequent pregnancies and by age. Further it is noticed that the ANC coverage also decreased progressively during the second and third trimesters. In other words, despite the efforts of social inclusion, the practice of social exclusion persists as far as antenatal care services are concerned.

ACCESS TO HEALTH SERVICES AND FACILITIES

The review of literature suggests that access to services has bearing on maternal health care and on reproductive health of women. For instance, Greene (2005), points out that currently there is much evidence to suggest that although access maybe increasing at a national level in some countries, access is not equal across different social groups. Poverty is a key factor excluding many from accessing services. For example, studies have found that access to a skilled birth attendant at delivery is over three times higher for women in the richest quintile than those in the poorest in sub-Saharan Africa, and eight times higher in South Asia (Greene, 2005). Hemminki (1997), also noted that access to care and the experience of treatment are also difficult among women in the lower socio-economic status (Hemminki, 1997). Similarly, Molesworth, K. (2005), observed that Poor communications and transport infrastructure can be important in preventing access to services in rural areas, especially in maternal health care where transport to referral services is an essential component of dealing with emergencies and preventing mortality.

Our analysis reveals that the health services of health professionals and medical facilities are accessible at a

Table 5.3.1: Reproductive Health Status: Social Exclusion.

	India	AP	Anantapur District	Total	Mala	Madiga	Adavi Golla	Boya	15-25	25-49
Mean age of Women at marriage	19.5	18.4	18.5	17.66	19.33	17.3	17.47	18.76	18.3	17.59
Percentage of women marrying below the legal age of 18 years	28.0	38.6	38.8	40.1	0	41.1	52.0	23.4	27.27	32.31
Age at first Birth	19.3	18.6	0	19.39	22.0	15.83	19.44	18.95	18.16	18.5
Percentage of women of 3+ children	42.0	22.5	21.7	38.8	23.3	33.3	41.0	36.7	6.06	52.15

1 age at first

2 median age at first birth women aged 25-49 – NHFS-3

Table 5.3.2: Reproductive Health Practices: Social Exclusion & Social Inclusion.

		India	AP	Anantapur District	Total	Mala	Madiga	Adavi Golla	Boya	15-25	25-45
Place of Delivery Percentage of Home deliveries	%	69.8	38.6	48.7	44.89	16.67	31.66	53.57	55.64	35.71	46.8
Institutional Deliveries (both Govt. & Pvt.)	%	29.8	60.9	50.4	55.11	83.33	68.33	46.42	44.36	64.29	53.19
Institutional (Govt.) Deliveries	%	15.0		28.0	31.86	16.67	25.0	41.66	30.88	31.75	32.8
Institutional (Pvt.) Deliveries	%	14.8		22.4	23.25	66.67	43.33	4.76	13.53	32.54	20.35
Delivery attendant by skilled persons either home/Institutional[1]	%	37.2	69.0	58.02	60.3	66.7	73.0	48.0	66.7		
Home delivery assisted by skilled persons	%	7.1	21.0	NA	NA	—	—	—	—		
Percentage of safe celivery[2]	%	47.6	69.0	73.5[3]	69.0	100.0	77.8	63.0	66.7		

[1] Doctor/Nurse/ANM.

[2] Deliveries assisted by skilled person both at home/institution.

[3] Delivery assisted by Doctor/Nurse/ANM/TBA.

reasonable distance for majority of the respondents and communities under reference. The only exception however, is Adavi Golla members. The gratifying feature is that a prepondering majority of Scheduled Caste members under reference have access to these facilities either within village or within a distance of two kilometers.

Our data shows that health worker/trained birth attendant is accessible within the village for 58.5 per cent of respondents. The services of ANM/Nurse can be availed by 49.8 per cent of respondents within the village. Only 18.8 per cent respondents can have access to Doctor within the village.

The data further reveals that none of the Adavi Golla members can avail the services of doctor within the village. To avail the services of doctor these members have to go beyond three kilometers (40.0 per cent) and six kilometers (40.0). 46.0 per cent of Madiga members and 33.3 per cent of Boya members can avail the services of doctor within the village. The services of doctor are available at distance of more than six kilometers for Madiga (15.9 per cent) Boya (23.3 per cent) and Adavi Golla (40.0).

The Adavi Golla members experience in availing the services of even Health Worker/Train Birth Attendant and ANM/Nurse. They are available at distance of more than three kilometers for these members. Majority of the Scheduled Caste members can avail the services of these members either within the village or within the reach of three kilometers. All the Boya members can avail the services of these members within the village itself.

Our data shows that government health facility can be availed by 13.1 per cent within the village; 34.9 per cent by at distance of within two kilometers and by at distance of more than six kilometers by 34.5 per cent. On the

Table 5.3.3: Maternal Health Care: Social Exclusion & Social Inclusion.

		India	AP	Anantapur District	Total	Mala	Madiga	Adavi Golla	Boya	15-25	25-45
1		2	3	4	5	6	7	8	9	10	11
1)Antenatal care											
1.1 Percentage of women that received on ANC check-up in the first Trimester of Pregnancy	%	40.2	66.5	96.7[1]	83.3	61.6	57.1	47.0	83.3	69.7	59.7
1.2 percentage of women that received three or more ANC checkups	%	50.0	87.9	87.3	59.9	66.7	49.2	41.0	86.0	59.1	55.02
1.3 percentage of women that received Full ANC*	%	16.4	43.9	47.2	48.0	83.3		42.0	50.0	57.6	45.5
2) Immunization											
2.1 Percentage of women that received at least one T.T. injection	%	80.0	87.9	88.5	75.0	16.7	90.5	75.0	65.0	87.9	

1		2	3	4	5	6	7	8	9	10	11
2.2 percentage of women that received 2 & more T.T. injection	%			88.5	17.0	83.3	12.7	17.0	15.0	37.9	26.05
3)IFA Supplementation											
3.1 Percentage of women that received adequate IFA tablets during pregnancy	%	20.4	48.3	50.3	72.9	100.0	85.7	56.0	85.0	84.8	68.02

* Full ANC =

contrary private health facility can be availed within the village by 34.5 per cent and within a distance of two kilometers by 48.0 per cent. Thus, private health facility is more easily accessible to the majority. A large percentage of Adavi Golla members do not have access to both government and private health facilities.

The services Anganwadi and Anganwadi Workers are however, available either within the village or at a distance of within two kilometers for all the communities.

Thus our data shows that as far as accessibility to services of grass-root health professionals is concerned, there is greater Social Inclusion. The only exception however is Adavi Golla members. This is partly due to their habitation settlements. The Adavi Golla lives in small hamlet villages which are located away at a distance from the main village thus resulting in social exclusion.

REFERENCES

Acsadi, George T.F., and Gwendolyn Johnson-Acsadi. 1990. Safe Motherhood in South Asia socio-cultural and demographic aspects of maternal health' Background Paper, Safe Motherhood South Asia Conference, Lahore.

Barata, Pedro., 2000. 'Social Exclusion in Europe: Survey of Literature' The Laidlaw Foundation.

Bhatia, J.C. 1988. 'A Study of Maternal Mortality in Anantapur District, Andhra Pradesh, India' Bangalore: Indian Institute of Management.

Bynner, John. 1998. 'Use of Longitudinal Data in the Study of Social Exclusion. OECD: Centre for Educational Research and Innovation. [http://www.oecd.org/els/edu/ceri/conf220299.htm]

De Haan, Arjan. 1998. 'Social Exclusion: An Alternative Concept for the Study of Deprivation?' pp.10-19 in IDS Bulletin, Vol. 29, No. 1.

District Level Health Survey (DLHS-2, 2002-04), 2006. "Reproductive and Child Health" International Institute of Population Sciences (Deemed University), Mumbai.

Health Canada. 2001. 'Social Capital, Social Cohesion, Social Inclusion/ Exclusion.' Population Health Newsletter. Ottawa.

Jo Beall and Laure-Hélène Piron. 2005. 'DFID Social Exclusion Review', The London School of Economics and Politcical Science.

Kapil, U., 1990. "Promotion of Safe Motherhood in India," Indian Pediatrics, 27: No. 3 (March), pp. 232-238.

Klasen, Stephan. 1998. 'Social Exclusion and Children in OECD Countries: Some Conceptual Issue',. OECD: Centre for Educational Research and Innovation. [http://www.oecd.org/els/edu/ceri/conf220299.htm]

Lieslie, Joanne., 1991. 'Women's Nutrition: the Key to Improving Health in Developing Countries,' Health Policy and Planning, No.1, pp.1-19.

Mathai, Sharmma, T. 1989, 'Women and the Health System' in C. Gopalan and Suminder Kaur (Eds.), Women and Nutrition in India, New Delhi, Nutrition Foundation of India.

National Family Health Survey (NFHS 3, 2005–06). 2007. International Institute of Population Sciences (Deemed University), Mumbai.

Nayar, K.R. 2007. 'Social Exclusion, Caste & Health: A Review Based on the Social Determinants Framework', Indian J. Med. Res. 126, pp. 355-363.

Noel L. Espallardo, 2004. Women's Sexual and Reproductive Health: Equity, Access and Quality in Family Practice', First Published 2004 by THE FAMILY MEDICINE RESEARCH GROUP, INC. Department of Family and Community Medicine, Taft Avenue, Manila, Philippines.

Philip O'Hara. 2006. 'Social Inclusion Health Indicators: A Framework for Addressing the Social Determinants of Health', Edmonton Social Planning Council, Edmonton.

Ramachandran, Prema., 1989. 'Lactation-nutrition-fertility Interaction', in C. Gopalan and Sluminder Kaur (Eds.), Women and Nutrition in India, New Delhi, Nutrition Foundation of India.

Registerar General, 1987. 'Survey of Causes of Deaths (Rural): Annual Report 1984 and 1986', A Report, Series 3, No.17 and 19, New Delh: Office of the Registrar General.

Royston, Eric and Sue Armstrong. 1989. 'Preventing Maternal Deaths', Geneva: World Health Organization.

UNICEF, India. 1991. 'Children and Women in India: A Situation Analysis,' New Delhi, UNICEF.

Wilkinson, R. and Marmot, M. 1998. 'Social Determinants of Health: The Solid Facts', World Health Organization, Copenhagen.

World Health Organization. 2005. 'Knowledge Network on Social Exclusion. Commission on the Social Determinants of Health Regional Consultation. Presentation. www.who.int/social-determinants.

CHAPTER 6

Summary and Conclusions

Reproductive Health in India is largely influenced by poverty-related and socio-culture factors on the one hand, and programme interventions on the other. Socio-cultural factors which impinge reproductive health include women's lack of awareness of health practices, strong seclusion norms which inhibit health-seeking, adolescent marriage, large family size norms which encourage frequent and closely spaced pregnancies, and a general devaluation of women which makes them the last to obtain food or health care and which requires of them long periods of physical activity.

Decades of research have shown that social exclusion impacts health and is aggravated by health status (World Health Organization, 2005).

To overcome social exclusion in the area of health, India adopted the development approach. In the development approach, improvement in health status is viewed primarily as a product of socio-economic development. By definition, development implies improved nutrition, hygienic living and working conditions, greater awareness of health problems and wider accessibility to health care services which have a favourable effect on the health status of the people. Improvements in health status as well as health care are treated as integrated components of the development process, in which medical care is just one of the many inputs; the impact of state intervention on health status depends on its overall socio-economic policies.

Accordingly, India during the past few years made a bold and impressive, determined and planned effort to empower health status of its populace. Over the years it has adopted a two faced strategy to usher social inclusion. On one hand it strived to achieve overall socio-economic development with equity to influence and enhance the health status; and on the other it has attempted to raise the health status independent of socio-economic development through State intervention by extending health care with equity. RCH was one such programme which was launched in the year 1997.

In view of the above reflections an attempt is made in this paper to study **the practices of social exclusion and achievements of social inclusion of reproductive health practices** of a backward, indigenous and traditional communities in a chronically drought prone and backward district.

The specific **objectives** of the study are:

a. To portray the socio-economic characteristics of selected backward, indigenous and traditional communities;

b. To analyze the access to communication, education & health services and facilities to the selected communities;

c. To examine the reproductive health status of the selected communities;

d. To analyze the reproductive health practices of the selected communities;

e. To obtain data on the indicators of reproductive health; and

f. To examine the practice of Social Exclusion and Social Inclusion in relation to the reproductive health care and practices of the communities under reference.

The study is carried out in the context of Anantapur District of Andhra Pradesh. The study sample comprises 229 households drawn from 19 villages representing five revenue mandals by adopting stratified random sampling technique. Interview schedule and focus group discussions were employed for the data collection.

MAJOR FINDINGS

The Setting

The study villages represent remotely located and backward revenue mandals of the district which is itself a chronically drought prone and backward district. One important feature is that most of the villages are hamlet villages which are constituent villages. Nine of the thirteen study villages are hamlet villages and four are main revenue villages.

SOCIO-ECONOMIC STATUS

Our study reveals that the respondents under reference were found to be relatively young women of below thirty five years, married, illiterate, involved in manual labour and poor.

The respondents represent Mala, Madiga, Adavigolla and Boya Caste Communities. Mala and Madiga belong to Scheduled Castes; and Adavi Golla, Boya Communities belong to Backward Castes. Traditionally, Madiga are leather workers, Adavigolla are Sheppards.

The average age of the respondents was found to be 31.4 years. However, 28.8 per cent of the respondents were found to be in the age group of 15 to 25 years; and only 5.67 were aged above 46 years.

The respondents are found to have small sized families. The average size of the family was found to be 4.76 members, which is smaller than the district's average size of five members.

Large sized families (8+ members) constitute only 5.1 per cent. Such families were found to be more among Adavi Golla and Boya Communities.

Majority of the respondents belong to nuclear families (71.6 per cent) and only 28.4 per cent belong to joint families.

Majority of the respondents are illiterates (62.8 per cent). The female illiteracy is found to be higher than the district's female illiteracy (59.1 per cent). Illiteracy was found to be highest among Adavi Golla (74.0 per cent) and Madiga (61.0 per cent) community members. It is found that only 12.7 per cent had ten and above years of school education.

The average annual income of the respondents was found to be only Rupees 8,439. Madiga Community women were found to earn the least incomes (Rs.7,440).

Large percentages (35.4 per cent) were found to be landless. 64.6 per cent do own land and are found to be marginal farmers having less than three acres of land.

A prepondering majority of the respondents (90.4 per cent) were found to be involved in manual agricultural labour as their primary occupation.

ACCESS TO HEALTH FACILITY AND SERVICES

Our analysis reveals that the health services of health professional and medical facilities are accessible at a reasonable distance for the majority of the respondents and communities under reference.

The only exception however is that of Adavi Golla members. The gratifying feature is that a prepondering majority of Scheduled Caste members under reference have access to these facilities either within village or within a distance of two kilometers. It is found that health worker/trained birth attendant is accessible within the village for 58.5 per cent of respondents. The services of ANM/Nurse can be availed by 49.8 per cent of respondents within the village. Only 18.8 per cent respondents can have access to doctor within the village.

It is found that none of the Adavi Golla members can avail the services of doctor within the village. To avail the services of doctor these members have to go beyond three kilometers (40.0 per cent) and six kilometers (40.0). The Adavi Golla members experience disadvantage in availing the services of even Health Worker/Train Birth Attendant and ANM/Nurse. They are available at distance of more than three kilometers for these members.

Forty six per cent of Madiga members and 33.3 per cent of Boya members can avail the services of doctor within the village. The services of doctor are available at distance of more than six kilometers for Madiga (15.9 per cent) Boya (23.3 per cent) and Adavi Golla (40.0).

Majority of the Scheduled Caste members can avail the services of these members either within the village or within the reach of three kilometers. All the Boya members can avail the services of these members within the village itself.

It is found that government health facility can be availed by 13.1 per cent within the village; by 34.9 per cent at distance of within two kilometers; and by 34.5 per cent at a distance of more than six kilometers. On the contrary private health facility can be availed within the village by 34.5 per cent and within a distance of two kilometers by 48.0 per cent. Thus, private health facility is more easily accessible to the majority.

A large percentage of Adavi Golla members do not have access to both government and private health facilities.

REPRODUCTIVE HEALTH STATUS

Marital Status

The proportion of women who are married and their ager structure has implications for policy-making and programme implementation.

In our study, it is found that marriage and marital status is universal among the Scheduled Castes and Backward Classes under study as against one-fifth women aged 15-49 years who were never married at all India level.

Considerable percentage (28.81 per cent) of women are found to be young and married (less than 25 years)

Age at Marriage

The legal age for girls marriage in India is 18 years. It is found that 40.17 per cent of women aged 15-49 years were married below the legal age; but among the younger population (15-25 years) it was found to be only 27.27 per cent.

The mean age at marriage however, was found to be 18.21 years for women aged 15-49 years and 18.63 years for women aged 15-25 years. The mean age at marriage was found to be lower than the legal age at marriage among the Madiga Community, which was 17.58 years.

The percentages of marriages below the legal age were found to more among Madiga (Scheduled Castes) Community (41.25 per cent) and Adavi Golla (Backward Class) Community (52.00).

Age at First Birth

First birth at adolescent age (< 18 years) is hazardous for women's reproductive health. Our study reveals an encouraging trend in this regard.

It is found that the mean age at first birth was 20.85 years and it is slightly lower (20.60 years) for the women aged 15-25 years. The mean age at first birth was found to be consistently above 20 years among all the caste groups under study.

However, it is found that 29.31 per cent women aged 15-25 years have given birth below the age of 18 years. The adolescents child births are found to be highest among Adavi Golla Community (38.00 per cent) followed by Madiga community (19.14 per cent).

Children Ever Born and 3+ Birth Order

Our study reveals that the number of children ever born varied by caste and age:

- It is found that the mean number of children born and living to the women aged 15-25 years was only 1.64 per cent and for the women aged 15-49 years 2.26 children.
- Among the women aged 15-25 years, the third order and plus number of births are found to be only 6.00 per cent.

- Third order and plus births are found to be 38.8 per cent among the women aged 15-49 years.
- Third order and above births are found to be highest among Mala Community (83.33 per cent) followed by Adavi Golla Community (41.0 per cent) and above 30 per cent in the case of Boya and Madiga Communities.

REPRODUCTIVE HEALTH PRACTICES

- Our study reveals an encouraging trend of progressive decline in the birth deliveries at home.
- It is found that deliveries at home have delivered to 24 per cent by third birth delivery.
- It is observed that while the importance of institutional deliveries is gaining greater acceptance, the credibility of government run health facilities is poor.
- Birth deliveries at home, it is found continue to be more among Backward Classes.
- The modern trained ANM, it is found is fast replacing the traditional mid-wife in assisting deliveries.
- Majority of the respondents (72.9 per cent) have received full IFA supplementation. But it is found this practice diminishes as the age and pregnancy order increases.
- Differential IFA acceptance levels among the castes under reference are observed. The supplementation of IFA is at low level among the Adavi Golla (40.0 per cent) than the other castes communities.
- Age and pregnancy order, caste differentials are found to be associated in the coverage of ANC services.
- It is found that younger mothers (15.25 per cent) of pregnancy have received greater attention with regard

to ANC. As the age, pregnancy order increases, the ANC services and acceptance had to as low as less than 30 per cent.

- The Scheduled Castes have been paid greater attention in the coverage of ANC services than the Backward Classes.
- Among the Backward Classes Adavi Golla are found to at a disadvantage in availing ANC service.
- The reach of ANC checkups and services during the third trimester is found to be poor, particularly during second and third pregnancy and thus escape the identification of risk factors.

REPRODUCTIVE HEALTH: SOCIAL EXCLUSION & SOCIAL INCLUSION

- Our study reveals that social exclusion in the form of adolescent marriages and adolescent child births persists among the communities which have greater involvement in the traditional agrarian and rural occupational structure. This trend is found to be in higher proportions in case of Madiga members (Scheduled Caste) and Adavi Golla Members (Backward Class).
- Social exclusion in the form of early marriages akin to adolescent marriage, is found to persist among Scheduled Caste Community of Madiga (41.1 per cent) and Backward Class Community Adavi Golla (52.00 per cent).
- Social exclusion in the form of adolescent child births is found to persist among Madiga Community. Among Madiga members the mean age at first birth is found to be 15.87 years.

- Social exclusion is found to be greater as the age and parity increases and persists among the Scheduled and Backward Classes. Antenatal care services, immunization, reduction of anemia still elude as more than forty per cent of women were not covered
- Our analysis reveals that the Backward Castes are at a disadvantage and experience social exclusion as far as birth delivery practices are concerned.
- The study also reveals emerging and encouraging trends of **social inclusion**. It is observed that by and large the deprivation/social exclusion of being married at a tender age is greatly reduced. This trend is evident from the declining percentage of women marrying below the legal age. It is found that among the respondents aged 15-25 years, only 27.27 per cent were married below the legal age.
- It is further observed that social inclusion in terms of acceptable mean age at first birth is gaining currency. The mean age at first birth among respondents is found to be 18.39 years and this trend is consistent among the most caste groups under reference.
- The social inclusion trends reveal that the efforts of district administration and health authorities and the strategy of imparting better health status independent of socio-economic and cultural status is rewarding enough.
- Our data shows that there is appreciable rise in the age at marriage and age at first birth and great reduction in **3^{+} births** particularly among the young women aged 15-25 years and among castes which do not have greater involvement in the agrarian/rural occupation structure.
- It is found that greater equity in health delivery is achieved in case of Scheduled Castes.

- Cent per cent of deliveries among Mala Community and 77.8 per cent of deliveries among Madiga Community were found to be safe deliveries, which are assisted by health professionals.
- Greater equity, however, is not found with regard to institutional deliveries. Only 55.11 per cent of birth deliveries found to be institutional deliveries; and such deliveries are found to be more common among the women aged 15-25 years (64.29 per cent) than the women higher age group (53.19 per cent).
- The gratifying feature however, is that there is greater social inclusion with regard to access to the grass-root health professionals and health facilities which are available within two kilometers. The only exception found to be Adavi Gollas and the reason is the nature of their habitat.

CONCLUSIONS

India has been making a bold attempt to provide reproductive health with equity and social inclusion to its massive populace independent of poverty and other socio-economic constraints. It has pursued a development approach after adopting a strategy of reproductive child health programme in 1997.

Based on the analysis and findings in the study an attempt is made to draw a few broad conclusions on the issues addressed.

Our first conclusion is that the strategy of RCH programme and the concept of reproductive health are facilitating greater social inclusion for the achievement of reproductive health with equity independent of socio-cultural constraints like poverty.

Higher age at marriage and first child birth, greater percentage of institutional births (deliveries), coverage of antenatal care services, access to grass-root health professionals, and health facility, to younger mothers (age 15-25 years) in particular and others (25>) in general among the poverty ridden Scheduled Caste and Backward Class members under study suggests social inclusion and provision of reproductive health with equity.

Notwithstanding the efforts and achievements of social inclusion in the area of reproductive health equity, our second conclusion is that social exclusion persists. Social exclusion practices are more in such reproductive health care areas as immunization, reduction of anemia, antenatal checkup services, identification of risk factors particularly during the third trimester of pregnancy, pregnancy complication, knowledge/awareness of reproductive track infections, and such social groups as older mothers (25> years age) with second and third pregnancies, women belonging to such occupational groups which are involved in agrarian rural occupation structure and Backward Classes.

Our third conclusion is that the persistence of social exclusion is more due to the lapses of monitoring and involvement of middle level/senior professionals/officers rather than access to health facility and grass-root heath professionals; and due to the failure of emphasis on advocacy and information education and communication (IEC) to sensitize these groups.

Women in general and women of the social groups mentioned above in particular are socialized in self-denial and modesty and hence are unlikely to acknowledge a health problem. Moreover, these groups consider child bearing and the related events normal process and part of a woman's life which do not deserve any special efforts and care. This is compounded by women's lack of autonomy and decision-making. Hence, the need for stress on advocacy and IEC.

Our fourth conclusion is that social exclusion practices observed in the reproductive health care area are of social relational and are passive. These are relational deprivations which can lead to very bad results. The deprivations come about through a social process in which there is no deliberate attempt to exclude, and therefore, the social exclusion can be considered, to use Amarthya Sen's classification, a "passive kind". This is of great instrumental importance for policy response.

Bibliography

Abel-Smith, B. 1978. 'Poverty, Development and Health Policy', WHO, Geneva.

Acsadi, George T.F., and Gwendolyn Johnson-Acsadi, 1990 'Safe Motherhood in South Asia Socio-cultural and Demographic Aspects of Maternal Health', Background Paper, Safe Motherhood South Asia Conference, Lahore.

Agarwal, D.K. and K.N. Agarwal, 1987. 'Early Childhood Mortality in Bihar and Uttar Pradesh', Indian Pediatrics, 24, No.8 (August): 627-32.

Agarwal, V., S. Patil and S. Khanijo, 1982. 'Study of Maternal Mortality', Journal of Obstetrics and Gynaecology 32, No.5 (October): 688-92.

Ananda Row, T. 1901. 'Census of India 1901', Vol. XXIV. Government Printing Press, Bangalore.

Ananthakrishna Iyer, L.K. 1930. 'The Mysore Tribes and Castes', The Mysore Government Press, Bangalore, Vol. III, pp.197-217.

Aras, R., N. Pai, and A. Purandare, 1990. 'Peri-natal Mortality – A Retrospective Hospital Study', Journal of Obstetrics and Gynaecology 40, No.3 (June): 365-69.

Aras, R., N. Pai, A, Baliga, S. Jain and Naimuddin 1989. 'Pregnancy a Teenage - Risk Factor for Lower Birth Weight', Indian Pediatrics 26, No. 8 (August): 823-25.

Arriaga, E.E. Davis, Kingsley. 1969. 'The Pattern of Mortality Change in Latin America,' Demography, Vol. 6, No. 3.

Banerji, D. 1980. 'Political Economy of Population Control in India' in L. Bondestan and S. Bergstrom, eds., Poverty and Population Control, Academic Press, London.

Barata, Pedro., 2000. 'Social Exclusion in Europe: Survey of Literature' The Laidlaw Foundation.

Baru, Rama V. 1987. 'Factors Influencing Variations in Health Services: A Study of Selected Districts of Andhra Pradesh', Unpublished M.Phil. Dissertation Submitted to the Jawaharlal Nehru University.

Benn, Hugo. 1979. 'Socio-Economic Determinants of Mortality in Latin America', in Proceedings of U.N.W.H.O. Conference on Socio-economic Determinants and Consequences of Mortality, Mexico.

Berger, J. 2004. 'Re-sexualizing the Epidemic: Desire, Risk and HIV Prevention', Development Update, 5(3), 45-67, Johannesburg.

Bhardwaj, N. et al., 1990. 'Socio-economic Factors Affecting Weight Gain in Pregnancy', Journal of Obstetrics and Gynaecology 40, No.3 (June): 327-30.

Bhatia, J.C. 1988. 'A Study of Maternal Mortality in Anantapur District, Andhra Pradesh, India-Bangalore: Indian Institute of Management.

Bynner, John. 1998. 'Use of Longitudinal Data in the Study of Social Exclusion, OECD: Centre for Educational Research and Innovation. [http://www.oecd.org/els/edu/ceri/conf220299.htm].

Carrin, G. 1984. 'Economic Evaluation of Health Care in Developing Countries: The Theory and Application', Croom Helm, London.

Cassen, Robert. 1976. 'Development and Population', Economic and Political Weekly, No. 31-33.

Chadha., 1963. 'Report of the Special Committee on Preparation for Entry NMEP into Maintenance Phase', Ministry of Health, Government of India.

Chadwick, E., 1956. 'Report on the Sanitary Conditions of the Labouring Population in Great Britain', Illustrations by M.W. Flinn, Reprinted of Edinburgh Press, (1882).

Chandrasekhar, M. and Balaji Prasad. 1997. 'Health Management – A System Approach', in Prof. G. Ramachandrudu ed., Health Planning in India, A.P.H. Publishing Corporation, New Delhi.

Chatterjee, Meera. 1989, 'Socio-economic and Socio-cultural Influences on Women's Nutritional Status Roles' in C. Gopalan and Suminer Kaur (eds.), Women and Nutrition in India, New Delhi: Nutrition Foundation of India.

Clancy C. and Massion C. 1992. 'American Women's Health Care: A Patchwork Quilt with Gaps', JAMA, 268: 1918-1920.

Coale, A.J. and Hoover, E.M. 1983. 'Population Growth and Economic Development in Low Income Countries', D.K. Agencies, New Delhi.

Cockerham, William, C. 1978. 'Medical Sociology', Prentice Hall International.

Cumper, G.E. 1987. 'Economic Development, Health Services and Health' in K. Lee and A. Mills, ed., The Economic of Health in Developing Countries, Oxford University Press, Oxford.

Cumper, G.E. 1984. Determinants of Health in Developing Countries, Letchworth: Hertfordshire, Research Studies Press Ltd.

Das Gupta, A.K. 1988. 'Growth, Development and Welfare', Basil Blackwell, Oxford.

Dawn, C.S. and Bani Kumar Mitra. 1990. 'Effect of Food Supplementation on Maternal Weight Gain, Low Birth Weight Incidence, Infant Weight Gain and Breast Feed Performance', Journal of Obstetrics and Gynaecology 40, No.3 (June): 313-18.

De Haan, Arjan. 1998. 'Social Exclusion: An Alternative Concept for the Study of Deprivation?' pp.10-19 in IDS Bulletin, Vol. 29, No. 1.

Department of Family Welfare, 'Basic Guide to Reproductive and Child Health Programme for use by NGOs, Training Institutions and Health Functionaries', New Delhi, Department of Family Welfare, Government of India.

Jo Beall and Laure-Hélène Piron. 2005. 'DFID Social Exclusion Review', The London School of Economics and Politcical Science.

District Level Health Survey (DLHS-2, 2002-04). 2006. 'Reproductive and Child Health' International Institute of Population Sciences (Deemed University), Mumbai.

Doyal, L. and Pennell, I. 1976. 'Health, Medicine and Underdevelopment', Economic and Political Weekly, No. 31-33.

Doyal, Lesley. 1979. 'The Political Economy of Health', The Pluto Press, London.

Dubos, Rene. 1960. 'Man, Medicine and Environment', Penguin, Harmondsworth.

Dubos, Rene., 1968. 'Medicine, Man and Environment', New York.

Dubos, Rene. 1959. ' Mirage of Health', Utopias, Progress and Political Change, New York.

Dubos, Rene. 1960. 'Pasteur and Modern Science', New York.

Durga Prasad, P. 1997. 'Socio-cultural Determinants of Health Status of Rural Women', in Prof. G. Ramachandrudu ed., Health Planning in India, A.P.H. Publishing Corporation, New Delhi.

Engles, F. 1978. 'The Conditions of the Working Class in England', Progress Publishers, Moscow.

Gopalan, C. 1989. 'Women and Nutrition in India –General Consideration,' in C. Gopalan and Suminder Kaur (eds.), Women and Nutrition in India, New Delhi: Nutrition Foundation of India.

Gopalan, C., 'Nutrition and Public Health: The Current Indian Scene', 13th Founder Memorial Lecture, Shri Ram Institute of Industrial Research, Delhi, 1977.

Government of India, "Health for All by 2000 AD Need for Comprehensive Evolution", Report, Vol. II, Manager of Publications, New Delhi, 1946.

Government of India, Report of the Health Survey on Planning Committee, Ministry of Health, New Delhi, 1962.

Green ME & Merrick T., 2005. 'Poverty Reduction: Does Reproductive Health Matter?', HNP Discussion Paper, World Bank, Washington DC.

Grosse, R.N. "Interrelation between Health and Population: Observation Derived from Field Experiences", Social Science and Medicine, Vol. 14c, No.2.

Hassan, S.S. 1920. 'Castes and Tribes of the H.E.H. The Nizam's Dominions Hyderabad State', The Times Press, Bombay.

Health Canada, 2001. 'Social Capital, Social Cohesion, Social Inclusion/Exclusion'. Population Health Newsletter. Ottawa

Central Bureau of Health Intelligence. 2003. 'Health Information of India', Directorate of General of Health Services, Ministry of Health and Family Welfare, New Delhi.

Hemminki E., Sihvo S., Koponen P. and Kosumen E. 1997, 'Quality of Contraceptive Services in Finland', Qual Health Care, 6:62-68.

Heptulla, Najma. 1997. Role of Empowerment of Women in Population Stabilization'. The Population Foundation of India, New Delhi, November 29.

Holla, M. 1985. 'Vital Statistics System - Major Source of Information on infant and Child Mortality', Indian Pediatris 52: 115-26.

Indian Council of Social Science Research and Indian Council of Medical Research. 1981. 'Health for All: An Alternative Strategy', Indian Institute of Education, Pune.

Iyengar, L. 1975. 'Influence of the Diet on the Outcome of Pregnancy in Indian Women', in Proceedings of the 9th International Congress of Nutrition, Mexico, 1972, Vol. 2, Karger, Nutrition, pp. 48-53.

Jain, M.L. and Dinesh Agarwal. 1986. 'Utilization of Maternal Services in an ICDS BLOCK', Journal of Obstetrics and Gynaecology 36, No. 5 (October): 842-44.

Jejeebhoy, Shireen J. and S. Rama Rao. 1992. 'Unsafe Motherhood: A Review of Reproductive Health in India. Paper Presented at the Workshop on Health and Development in India, Sponsored by the National Council of Applied Economic Research and Harard University, Centre for Population and Development Studies, New Selhi, 2-4 January.

Jo Beall and Laure-Hélène Piron. 2005 'DFID Social Exclusion Review', The London School of Economics and Political Science.

Kamalajayaram, V. and T. Parameswari, 1988. 'A Study of Septic Abortion Cases in the Last 6 Years', Journal of obstetrics and Gynaecology 38, No. 4 (August): 389-92.

Kanitkar, Tara and R.K. Sinha, 1989. 'Antenatal Care Services in Five States of India'. In S.N. Singh, M.K. Premi, P.S./ Bhatia and Ashish Bose (eds.), Population Transition in India, Vol. 2, pp. 201-11, Delhi: B.R. Publishing Corporation.

Kapil, U., 1990. 'Promotion of Safe Motherhood in India,' Indian Pediatrics, 27: No.3 (March): pp. 232-238.

Kelman, S. 1975. 'The Social Nature of Definition Problems of Health', International Journal of Health Services, 5(4), 65-42.

Khan, M.E. and C.V.S. Prasad. 1983. Under-utilization of Health Services in Rural India: A Comparative Study of Bihar, Gujarat and Kerala, Baroda: Operations Research Group.

Khan, M.E., Richard Anker, S.K. Ghosh Dastidar and Sashi Airathi. 1988. 'Inequalities between Men and Women in Nutrition and Family Welfare Services: an in-dept enquiry in an Indian Village', Social Action 38, (October-December).

Kholi, K.L. 1977. 'Mortality in India: A State-wise Study, Sterling', New Delhi.

Kielman, A.A. and Oberoi, I.S., Interaction of Nutrition and Infection: A Prospective Field Study on Children TB Programme in India, Final Report to ICMR, Rural Health Research Centre, Ludhiana, 1972.

Klasen, Stephan. 1998. 'Social Exclusion and Children in OECD Countries: Some Conceptual Issue',. OECD: Centre for Educational Research and Innovation. [http://www.oecd.org/els/edu/ceri/conf220299. htm]

Kondala Rao, K.N. 1997. 'Selective Primary Health Care (A Case of Universal Immunization Programme)', in Prof. G. Ramachandrudu ed., Health Planning in India, A.P.H. Publishing Corporation, New Delhi.

Krishnan, P. 1975. 'Mortality Decline in India, 1951-196: Development Versus Public Health Programme Hypotheses', Social Science and Medicine, Vol.19.

Kuhn, Thomas S., 1970. 'The Structure of Scientific Revolutions, Chicago, Chicago University Press', 2nd Edition.

Kumar, Harsh, S. Aneja, V.K. Prasad, S.K. Arora and D.N. Mulick. 1988. 'Tetanus Neonatorum: Clinico-epidemiologicla Profile', Indian Pediatrics 25, No.11 (November): 1054-1057.

Kumar, Vijay and Inderjit Walia. 1983. 'Beliefs and Practices of Birth Attendants during Antenatal Period in a Rural Area' Journal of Obstetrics and Gynaecology 33, No. 4 (August): 460-65.

Le Grand, Julian. 1982.' The Strategy of Equality: Redistribution and the Social Services', George Allen and Unwin, London.

Lieslie, Joanne., 1991. "Women's Nutrition: The Key to Improving Health in Developing Countries", Health Policy and Planning, No.1, pp.1-19.

Malathi, M.S., 1993. 'Medical Sociology: Social Epidemiology and Illness Behaviour', Unpublished Ph.D. Thesis submitted to Sri Krishnadevaraya University, Anantapur.

Mathai, Sharmma, T. 1989, "Women and the Health System" in C. Gopalan and Suminder Kaur (Eds.), Women and Nutrition in India, New Delhi, Nutrition Foundation of India.

Matthews, Z., Ramakrishna, J., Mahendra. S., Kilaru, A., and Ganapathy, S. 2005. 'Birth Rights and Rituals in Rural South India: Care Seeking in the Intrapartum period', Journal of Biosocial Science, 37(4), 385-411.

Mckinlay, J. & Mckinlay, S. 1977. The Questionable Contribution of Medical Measures to the Decline of Mortality in 20th Century, Milbank Memorial Fund Quarterly, Vol. 55.

Mehta, A. and K. Jayant. 1981. 'Parinatal Mortality Survey in India (1977-79), Part I, Identification of Health Intervention Needs', Journal of Obstetric Gynaecology 32, No.2 (April): 183-215.

Mehta, A. M.E. Khan, R.B. Gupta, M.M. Gandotra and O.S. Ojha. 1983. 'Role of Health Services Delivery on Acceptance of Family Planning, New Delhi: ICMR, Mimeo.

Mehta, S.R., 1984. 'Society and Health: A Sociological Perspective', Vikas Publishing House.

Mensch, B., J. Bruce and B Greene. 1998. 'The Uncharted Passage: Girls' Adolescents in the Developing World, Population Council, New York.

Merrick. 1985.'The Effect of Piped Water on Early Childhood Mortality Rates in Urban Brazil, Demography', Vol. 22, 1-23.

Michels T. 2000. 'Patients Like Us: Pregnant and Parenting Teens View the Health Care System', Public Health Rep, 115: 557-575.

Ministry of Health and Family Welfare (MOH & FW), 1997. 'Statement of National Population Policy, New Delhi: Government of India.

Ministry of Welfare, Dept. of Women and Child Development, 1991. '15th year of ICDS, An Overview, New Delhi: Government of India.

Molesworth K., 2005. 'The Impact of Transport Provision on Direct and Proximate Determinants of Access to Health Services', Swiss Tropical Institute.

Morris, M.D., Measuring the Condition of the World Poor: The Physical Quality of Life Index, Pergamon Press Oxford, 1979.

Mukherjee, Reports on Reorganization of Family Planning Services Administration and Basic Health Services, Ministry of Health & Family Welfare, Government of India, 1966.

Murphy EM, Greene ME, Mihailovic A., Olupot-Olupot P. 2006. 'Was the "ABC" Approach (abstinence, being faithful, using condoms) Responsible for Uganda's Decline in HIV?', PLoS Med. 3(9): e379. DOI: 10.1371/journal.pmed.0030379.

Murthy, G.V., Anil Goswami and Saroja Narayanan. 1990. 'Utilization Patterns of Antenatal Services in an Urban Slum', Journal Obestetrics and Gynaecology 40, No.1 (February): 42-46.

Nag, Moni. 1983. 'Impact of Social and Economic Development on Mortality: Comparative Study of Kerala and West Bengal', Economic and Political Weekly, No. 19, 20, 21.

Nagaraju, K. 2005. 'Health Status of India: A Comparison of Selected States' Unpublished M.Phil. dissertation submitted to Sri Krishnadevaraya University, Anantapur, Andhra Pradesh.

Nagaraju, K. 2007. 'Dalits and Adolescent Sexual Health: Issues and Practices: A Study of De-notified Tribes, Scheduled Castes and Backward Caste Communities in Andhra Pradesh', Paper Presented to the Workshop for Young Social Scientists, Jammu.

Nanjundayya, H.V. and Ananthakrishna Iyer, L.K. 1931. 'The Mysore Tribes and Castes, The Mysore University, Mysore, Vol. IV, pp.125-169.

Narayana, K.V., Public Expenditure on Health in India: Trends and Priorities, Unpublished M.Phil. dissertation, Centre of Social Medicine and Community Health, JNU, New Delhi, 1981.

Narayana, K.V. 1997. Health and Development, Rawat Publication, Jaipur.

National Family Health Survey of India (NFHS-3). 2007. International Institute of Population Sciences (Deemed University), Mumbai.

National Family Health Survey of India (NHFS-1), 1992-93. International Institute for Population Sciences (Deemed University), Bombay.

National Family Health Survey of India (NHFS-2), 1998-99. International Institute for Population Sciences (Deemed University), Bombay.

Nayar, K.R. 2007, 'Social Exclusion, Caste & Health: A Review Based on the Social Determinants Framework' Indian J. Med. Res. 126, October, pp. 355-363

Noel L. Espallardo, 2004. "Women's Sexual and Reproductive Health: Equity, Access and Quality in Family Practice", First Published 2004 by The Family Medicine Research Group, Inc. Department of Family and Community Medicine, Taft Avenue, Manila, Philippines.

Pang Ruyan. 2001. 'The Important Issues in Developing a National Plan on Maternal Mortality. Department of Reproductive Health and Research'. WHO.

Panikar, P.G.K. and Soman, C.R. 1984. 'Health Status of Kerala: Paradox of Economic Backwardness and Health', Centre for Development Studies, Trivendrum.

Panikar, P.G.K. 1975. 'Fall in Mortality in Kerala: An Explanatory Hypothesis', Economic and Political Weekly, No. 47, 1811.

Parsons, T. 1972. 'Definitions of Health and Illness in the Light of American Values and Social Structure', in Jaco, E.G. Ed. Patients, Physicians and Illness, New York, The Free Press Glenco, and London Collier Macmillan.

Philip O'Hara. 2006. 'Social Inclusion Health Indicators: A Framework for Addressing the Social Determinants of Health,' Edmonton Social Planning Council, Edmonton.

Pittman. 1999. 'Gendered Experiences for health care', Int. J. Qual Health Care, 11:397-405.

Premi, M.K. 1997. 'Some Issues in Attaining Health for All', in Prof. G. Ramachandrudu ed., Health Planning in India, A.P.H. Publishing Corporation, New Delhi.

Preston, Samuel H. 1980. 'Causes and Consequences of Mortality Declines in Less Developed Countries during the Twentieth Century', in R.A. Esterlin, ed., Population and Economic Change in Developing Countries, The University of Chicago Press, Chicago.

Qadeer, Imrana. 1987. 'Giving Public Health Services More than Their Dues', Economic and Political Weekly, Vol. XXII, No. 29.

Ractiffe, John, 1978. 'Social Justice and the Demographic Transition: Lessons from India's Kerala State', International, Journal of Health Services; Vol. 8, No.1.

Ramachandran, Prema., 1989. 'Lactation-nutrition-fertility Interaction', in C. Gopalan and Sluminder Kaur (Eds.), Women and Nutrition in India, New Delhi, Nutrition Foundation of India.

Ramachandrudu, G. and Kamalamma, G. 1997. 'Health Planning in India - A Critical Evaluation', in Prof. G. Ramachandrudu ed., Health Planning in India, A.P.H. Publishing Corporation, New Delhi.

Ramachandrudu, G. and Venkata Rao G. 1997. 'Inter-district Variations in Health Services in Andhra Pradesh', in Prof. G. Ramachandrudu ed., Health Planning in India, A.P.H. Publishing Corporation, New Delhi.

Ramachandrudu, G. 1997. 'Health Planning in India', A.P.H. Publishing Corporation, New Delhi.

Ramalingaswami, V. 1985. 'The State of Life: Report of the National Seminar on Reducing Incidence of Low Birth Weight Babies in India, New Delhi: National Institute of Public Cooperation and Child Develop-ment.

Ramalingaswamy, V. 1975. 'Medicine, Health and Human Development', Ninth Jawarhalal Memorial Lecture, Jawaharlal Nehru Memorial Fund, New Delhi.

Rami Reddy, V., Gunasundaramma, G.P. Naidu, B.K.C Reddy and K.R.S. Reddy, 1980. 'ABO and Rh(D) Blood Groups in Ten Population of Sri Venkateswara University Area, South India', Indian Journal of Heredity, 12(3), pp.71-119.

Rani Gopal, K. 1997. 'Health Transition and the Role of Literacy', in Prof. G. Ramachandrudu ed., Health Planning in India, A.P.H. Publishing Corporation, New Delhi.

Register General, 1987. 'Survey of Causes of Deaths (Rural): Annual Report, 1984 and 1986', A Report, Series 3, Nos.17 and 19, New Delh: Office of the Registrar General.

Renaud, M., 'On the Structural Constraints to State Intervention in Health, International Journal of Health Services', 79(2), Papers and Proceedings, 1989, 337-42.

Rodgers, G.B., 'Income and Inequality as Determinants of Mortality: An International Cross-section Analysis', Population Studies, Vol. 9, No.1.

Royston, Eric and Sue Armstrong. 1989. 'Preventing Maternal Deaths', Geneva: World Health Organization.

Sadik, Jafis, 1980. 'Family Planning: Improving the Health of Women', Draper Fund Report, 9 (October).

Sagan, Leonard A. 1987. 'The Health of the Nations: True Causes of Sickness and Well-being', Basic Books, New York.

Sanders, David, 'The Struggle for Health', Macmillan, London.

Sen A. 1999. 'Development as Freedom'. New Delhi: Oxford University Press.

Sharma, N. and P. Bali. 1989. 'A Comparative Study of Maternal Mortality and Morbidity in a Teaching Hospital of Northern India', Journal of Obstetric and Gynacology, 38, No.2 p.177-181.

Singh Meharban, and V.K. Paul. 1988. 'Strategies to Reduce Perinatal and Neonatal Mortality', Indian Ediatrics 23, No.6 (June): 499-509.

Singh, K.S. 1998. 'India's Communities', Oxford University Press, New Delhi, Vol. V.

Singh, K.S. 1998. 'India's Communities', Oxford University Press, New Delhi, Vol. IV.

Singh, Meharban. 1986. 'Hospital Based Data on Perinatal and Neonatal Mortality in India,' Indian Pediatrics 23, No.8 (August): 579-584.

Singh, Surinder, Jagieet Singh, Sushila Mittal, R.K.D. Goel, Tejbir Singh and S.K. Oberoi. 1988. 'A Study of Antenatal Services in Rural Areas of District of Bathinda of Punjab', Journal of Obsetrics and Gynaecology 38, No.1 (February); 2-26.

Sokhy, J. 1988. 'Magnitude of Problems in India', in Ministry of Health and Family Welfare, The Control of Neonatal Tetanus in India, pp. 16-23, New Delhi, Government of India, Quoted in Singh and Paul.

Srikantia, S.G. 1989a. 'Nutritional Deficiency Diseases', in C. Gopalan and Suminder Kaur (eds.), Women and Nutrition in India, New Delhi: Nutrition Foundation of India.

Starrs, Ann and Diane Measham. 1990, 'Challenge for the Nineties: Safe Motherhood in South Asia', New York and Washington: The World Bank and Family Care International.

Suresh Kulkarni. 1992. 'Health for Peace', Northern Book Centre, New Delhi.

Thruston, E. 1909. 'Castes and Tribes of Southern India', Madras: Government Press, Madras; Rpt. 1975, Cosmo Publications, Delhi), Vol. II, pp. 284-295.

Thruston, E., 1909. 'Castes and Tribes of Southern India' Madras: Government Press, Madras; rpt. 1975; Cosmo Publications, Delhi), Vol. VI, pp.292-325.

Thruston, E., Castes and Tribes of Southern India (Madras: Government Press, 1090; Rpt. 1975, Delhi; Cosmo Publications), Vol. I.

Tripathi, A.M., D.K. Agarwarl, K.N. Agarwal, R.R. Devi and S. Cherian. 1987. 'Nutritional Status of Rural Pregnant Women and Foetal Outcome', Indian Pediatrics 24, No.9 (September): 703-712.

Umamohan, Ch., A. Naganna, K. Nagaraju, 2007. Reproductive Health Care: Intergenerational Study of Yerukala Tribe in Rayalaseema Region, in NOMADS, Prof. B.S. Vasudeva Rao (ed.), Andhra University Press, Visakhapatnam, Andhra Pradesh, pp.130-137.

UNICEF, India. 1984, 'An Analysis of the Situation of Children in India', New Delhi.

UNICEF, India. 1991, "Children and Women in India: A Situation Analysis", New Delhi, UNICEF.

United Nations. 1975. 'Poverty, Unemployment and Development Policy: A Case Study of Selected Issues with Reference to Kerala', UN, New York.

United Nations. 1962. 'The U.N. Development Decade: Proposals for Action, U.N. Publications', New York.

Virchow, R., Disease. 1981. 'Life and Man', Sanford University Press, Sanford, cited in H. Waitzkin, "The Social Origins of Illness: A Neglected History", International Journal of Health Services.

Waitzkin, H.B. and Waterman, B. 1974. 'The Exploitation of Illness in Capital Societies, Indianapolis.

Weisman., 2000. "The Trends in Health Care Delivery for Women: Challenge for Medical Education," Acad Med., 75: 1107-1113.

Wellings K., Wadsworth J., Johnson A., Field J., Macdowall W. 1999 'Teenage Fertility and Life Chances Teenage Fertility and Life Chances.' Rev. Report Sep; 4(3):184-90.

Wilkinson, R. and Marmot, M. 1998. 'Social Determinants of Health: The Solid Facts', World Health Organization, Copenhagen.

World Health Organization. 1974. "Special Subject: Health and Priorities, 1950-2000", World Statistical Report.

World Health Organization (WHO), 1994. 'Health, Population and *Development and Development*', WHO Position Paper for the International Conference on Population and Development, Cairl, WHO/FHE/94.I, Geneva, World Health Organization.

World Health Organization (WHO), 1957. 'Measuring Levels of Health, WHO Technical Report, No. 137, WHO, Geneva.

World Health Organization. 2005. 'Knowledge Network on Social Exclusion. Commission on the Social Determinants of Health Regional Consultation. Presentation. www.who.int/social-determinants

Zurayk, H.H. *et al.*, 1993. 'Concepts and Measures of Reproductive Morbidity, Health Transition Review, 3(1):17-39.

Index